VOYAGE NOT COMPLETED

VOYAGE
NOT
COMPLETED

Rupert Grayson

MACMILLAN

© Rupert Grayson 1969

First published in 1969 by

MACMILLAN AND CO LTD
Little Essex Street London WC2
and also at Bombay Calcutta and Madras
Macmillan South Africa (Publishers) Pty Ltd Johannesburg
The Macmillan Company of Australia Pty Ltd Melbourne
The Macmillan Company of Canada Ltd Toronto
Gill and Macmillan Ltd Dublin

Printed in Great Britain by
ROBERT MACLEHOSE AND CO LTD
The University Press, Glasgow

This book is dedicated to the masters and companies on whose ships I have enjoyed hospitality for many voyages.

Eden, CAPTAIN RATCLIFF, *Royal Mail,* Caribbean; **London Banker,** CAPTAIN NELSON, *London & Overseas Freighters,* China Seas; **Mahanada,** CAPTAIN BRIGGS, *Brocklebanks,* Indian Ocean; **Newfoundland,** CAPTAIN SHEFFIELD, M.B.E., *Furness Withy,* North Atlantic; **Overseas Courier,** CAPTAIN MACKENZIE, *London & Overseas Freighters,* Gulf of Mexico; **Stonepool,** CAPTAIN CHURCHILL, *Ropners,* Caribbean; **Gorey,** CAPTAIN FREEMAN, *Grandport Shipping Company,* Mediterranean.

Contents

ACKNOWLEDGEMENTS

Acknowledgement is due to H.R.H. The Duke of Windsor for graciously allowing us to reprint the letter which appears on pages 84–5, and to Mr Nicholas Monsarrat and Messrs Cassell & Co. Ltd for permission to reprint the passage from *Life is a Four-Letter Word* which appears on pages 142–5.

I

An Excellent Start in Life

I HAD tipped my porter generously (let there be one man to speak well of me when I am gone), and my 'crossed' Foreign Office bags were safely and conveniently stowed away. My suitcase on the rack above contained my personal belongings, including 'Cadette', my small radio. Though the train was crowded, I was alone in the compartment. The doors were locked, and I was well guarded.

Top-secret documents were concealed within a travelling-rug, rolled inside a canvas bag studded with brass-rimmed holes. If it became necessary to travel by sea and the ship was to founder, the bag, well-leaded, would sink without trace. No enemy would decipher my documents, and no enemy would warm himself under my rug. I was a middle-aged King's Messenger off on a routine job. I hung up my Harris tweed overcoat; it had a tangy smell, as if during the weaving a heather sprig had been caught in the loom.

Now, framed in the carriage window, the Kentish countryside flowed past, and I saw the twilight spreading over the fields. It was June, the month of nightingales and roses, and suddenly the smell of new-mown hay drifted into the compartment and I was a boy again in the first decade of the century, standing at the lodge-gates of our summer home in Flintshire, facing the farm.

I certainly made an excellent start in life, as they say, for I was born into a wealthy and loving family; and, if the spoon in my mouth was not pure silver, it was surely most richly plated.

I have eleven brothers and sisters – Denys the first-born, Ailsa the fair, Nancy the dark, Brian, Tristram, Auriol, Monica, Meryl,

Angela and, lastly, the twins Ambrose and Godfrey. In those days we had so much of everything: toys, tears, love and laughter. The stream of life flowed evenly, summers were long and hot, winters short with ice and snow. It was always someone's birthday, and, however tall we grew, the Christmas-tree grew higher still, with the decorations more exciting and the presents packed in bigger boxes, and over all the smell of pine and candle-wax.

In our brother-and-sisterhood we were complete in ourselves, inviolate and impregnable, leading our own secret lives with our own secret language, a world in which our parents, however much we loved them, were never a part. To this day in the company of others our eyes will meet, and even with no words we know what the other is thinking. Like most large families, we would all talk at the same time, and silence fell only when Father suggested we should speak in turn.

One part of the house was set aside for the current invalid, for we were regularly visited by chicken pox, measles, mumps and other afflictions, which usually took us each in turn. During these periods Father left for destinations unknown. He could be friendly with our doctor over a glass of port and uncommonly pleasant to attractive hospital nurses; but he had a horror of illness and everything to do with it.

When Brian had diphtheria at Aberduna, Father immediately left the house; but not before the mattress, with the sheets and blankets the invalid had used, had been burned in the stable-yard. Father tended to look on illness as a display of weakness by its victim. On board ship, no matter how bad the weather, we were forbidden to be sick. At any sign of our disobeying these orders we would be made to run round the decks until we were too exhausted to do anything but sleep.

We were a fiercely loving, undisciplined horde of savages. From cradle to saddle we had too many nannies and servants to do things for us. We dropped things when we had finished with them, and nannies (like caddies) teed them up again, so that we were never short of something to lose in the rough. Our nannies were invariably French, rosy and brown-eyed, and Mother always said that the first intelligible words we spoke were in French. 'Sur le pont d'Avignon' was the first song we learned to sing, and 'Notre Père' the first prayer we learned to say. We were not always as considerate to our nannies as we should have been. Strength, we had learned, lay in unity. We worked in a pack; the strongest nannie could be overcome by force of numbers. Thirty years later, crouched on the veld at Kazuma Pan in Southern Rhodesia, I saw a lioness harried from a drinking-pool by a pack of wild dogs. The motto under our coat of arms is aptly: 'Virtus tutissima turris' (roughly translated 'Strength is safest in a tower'). It was said that the name of Grayson was known throughout Brittany, and in the little coastal villages it was spoken only with hushed breath; yet from France there was always a fresh recruit ready to cross the Channel and engage in combat with us. Looking back, it seems as though we had always just seen off a Jeanne, a Marie or an Yvonne: we watched her pack her trunks with our presents and, as she departed, wept at the drive gates.

Our darling Mother was never in despair: she had long realised that her business lay not so much in keeping the nannies, which was clearly impossible, but rather in constantly finding fresh ones. She was in the same predicament as a general, hard pressed in battle, who awaits in anxious expectation the arrival of reinforcements.

Uncle Ambrose, a Royal Horse Artilleryman, who was killed in August 1914, had a way of breaking into verse for our amusement. He acted as children's jester at Mother's court. He suggested that she should always engage two for every one required.

> 'The nursery maid, when good, of course,
>   Is the very acme of resource.
> The one you want works like a horse,
>   Without ever feeling fainty.'

These young French girls delighted me: already I was beginning to look for the expression in their eyes.

Mother might be embroidering initials on towels for school when we returned from saying good-bye to one of the nannies.

Time and dates have never meant much to me, but towels and
handkerchiefs warned me clearly that preparations for school
were afoot. Then I would turn to the more remote places in the
garden in search of solitude: our home might have been designed
for this purpose.

Aberduna Hall stood in a fold of the Welsh hills, with black
sentinel woods imprisoning the house on three sides. On the
fourth the drive described a wide circle as it cut through an acre
of ancient turf. White iron gates led into a lane that descended a
hundred yards and then turned, left for Mold and right for
Marsavon. The farm buildings clustered round the gates, and
when the wind blew from the north the smell of cow-dung and
sweet hay seeped into our bedrooms.

Moel Vindick was a steep craggy hill that faced the house, or
possibly it was the house that faced Vindick; our eyes were
seldom turned away from it, for Vindick dominated our lives.
It was the barometer by which our days were planned. When
Vindick smiled we knew the picnic baskets could be packed, but
when Vindick frowned we were warned not to go beyond the
garden. My sisters (inclined to stray like the sheep) were dressed
in scarlet capes with bonnets laced with ribbon that tied under
the chin: thus they could be seen between the trees, or espied as
red dots on the distant mountainside. Vindick started at its base
with friendly fields, then came a layer of bracken, then one of
tangy heather, all ending in a rocky summit hewn like a mastiff's
head. Vindick held out longest against the twilight, and on its
eastern side the morning light climbed daily to its crown. It
could never stay the clouds, but it never failed to warn us; and,
when it did, sure enough, the lightning would flash, and we
would hear the thunder rolling down the valley.

One side of the estate was flanked with disused mine-shafts
that lay hidden, masked dangerously by the undergrowth, traps
for man and beast. Sometimes we would lie on the rotten wood,
slippery sleepers condemned by the railways and carelessly
thrown across the shafts. From this position, with the acrid
smell of nettles in our nostrils, we could peer down into the
darkness. For me the smell of nettles is for ever associated with

roots and depths. We would drop stones down the shaft, listening to their clackety-clack as they ricocheted from side to side, and wait with held breath for the final subterranean splash of waters that echoed, it seemed, from its bowels.

We slept in ship's bunks, and standing on the topmost we could see over the trees to the point where the lane emerged from the woods. As evening approached we watched for Father from our bedroom windows. He would be coming home from his shipyards on the Mersey. The gig would have met him at the station and brought him home up the eight steep miles of hill. His arrival was the most important moment of the day. We knew that he had walked the decks of many ships, that his eyes had seen a hundred foreign flags. He came from a city of tall masts and smoking funnels, from a riverside of docks and cranes and the strident music of clanging rivets and whining winches. He was a natural story-teller and when he told his stories it was the only time in the day when the pack was silent. He particularly liked telling of mysterious and strange happenings, and he had the gift of sending our minds dreaming along the corridors of history.

To our delight he never left out details: it was not enough that his hero had dined; we would be told what he had eaten and the name and vintage of the wines that he had drunk. It was from Father that we first learned the life-giving pleasure of French wines, the reds and the whites, though we ourselves were made to mix our wine with water, something that was never done by D'Artagnan or any other gentleman of France riding up from Gascony under the warm skies of Languedoc on the straight road that led to Paris and adventure.

The stories he told us were usually about brave men and beautiful women and strange meetings at the inn. It was never difficult to hear the rumble of coaches on the lonely road and the hoarse cry in the night: 'Stand and deliver, your money or your life!' Or the angry shout: 'Head them off at the cross-roads.' He illuminated life for us.

If any of us boys had been naughty during the day Father would be told of it on his return. In his shoe-cupboard he kept an old ping-pong bat, and, though seldom used, 'the bat' in Father's dressing-room was a silent reminder of what might befall our backsides if we misbehaved.

In those days the mail from Mold to Ruthin was carried at the fall of night in a coffin-shaped vehicle drawn by four horses. The driver and his guard crouched in a hooded seat: we were told that they carried whips with leaded lashes to slash off night-thieves. As a treat we were sometimes taken to see it pass. From the end of our lane we could just hear the sound of the hoof-beats as the horses swung down the hill from the village. If it was late, this was the signal for us to race to the main road. Arrived there, we would see in the distance a black patch darker than the night, pointed by twin orange lights that grew bigger every moment, while sparks from the iron-shod hoofs starred the road. The dark shadow came nearer and nearer until we could make out the rounded hood and hear the crack of the whip. Suddenly the swaying shadow was upon us, with a great metallic clattering on the hard road, the grinding of springs, the flick of bridle and reins, a champing and pungent smell of sweating horses. The next moment it had passed.

We had sensed rather than seen the muffled faces of the driver and his mate. Sometimes they must have seen our small excited faces peering up, illumined for a second in the lamplight; and above the jangle and grinding we would hear the sing-song shout of an alien tongue.

Welsh was spoken by all the people around Aberduna, spoken through the gaps in their teeth rather than their lips, for it was unusual to see anyone with teeth in even moderately good condition. In those days the villages were long distances in both miles and time from the towns, and there was no Health Service to encourage the peasantry to acquire dentures. Mother used to corner each of us once every holiday; then, after she had bribed us with a promise of a present – a pair of spurs, a Winchester rifle or a new saddle – we would be taken to the big city where our dentist lived.

He was a gentle torturer with soft, podgy hands and a spotlessly white, evenly starched coat. He worked in a street of doctors and

dentists in Liverpool known as The Valley of the Shadow of
Death. When I put my head back I looked up into a beautiful
waxed moustache and a pair of downcast beady eyes. Ailsa, who
was already twelve, constantly boasted that she was in love with
him. Mother was insistent about these visits, for she distrusted
school cooking, and she was determined to send us out into
the great world fully armed dentally. She herself had beautiful
teeth and could have bitten through a pencil at any time of the
day. Perhaps she did, for she seldom had a pencil out of her hand.
There were always people to whom she had to write, and she
seldom wrote in ink. Constant travelling with Father had conditioned her writing: the rat-tat of the wheel-joints, the grinding
bogies of the London North-Western Railway and the Paris–
Lyon–Méditerranée, had transformed her schoolgirl copperplate
into a lively, spiky, firm, bold hand.

Father, like a child, was never happy without his box of bricks
or his parcel of planks. There were always ship's carpenters,
bricklayers and electricians at Aberduna Hall, at High Meadow
and later at Ravenspoint. Cottages were always being built or
walls going up. At Aberduna Father had raised what he called
'tea-houses'. They were teak-built summer-houses strong enough
to ride a hurricane, designed to open on all sides and to close up
completely in bad weather. They were scattered about the woods,
so as to offer speedy shelter when a sudden storm blew up. If we
were off the estate there was always the village, with a choice of
little cottages where we were ever welcome. Aberduna to our
young minds was a place of mystery and storms.

The lane to the village pierced a wood darkly, like a tunnel,
but the short cut was the path that skirted the fields, ran over the
hill and leapt the stiles. We preferred this second route, because
it led ultimately to the village sweet-shop. On the way a call was
usually made at a small cement works, where Mr Radley, the
manager, presided. He was one of our childhood heroes. I
remember him as an enormous man, not straight and tall and
sun-tanned like Father, but big in a rotund way, probably five
foot five from the top of his hat to the soles of his boots. He had
popping blue eyes like a china doll and bulging red cheeks.

Mr Radley's moustache – unlike Father's, which was fair and
guardsmanlike – was blue-black, parted in the middle, and over-
hung his mouth in majestic curves. His flesh was non-porous and
highly polished, like the reflective patina of old rosewood or the
glow on a Ribston pippin.

It was from his office we noticed that our nurses used to find it
convenient to telephone. Telephone whom? It suited us admir-
ably, since Mr Radley never failed to send his assistant to buy
sweets from the little shop just over the brow of the hill; while
he gallantly took Jeanne or Marie into his sanctum to assist her
with the instrument. Those telephone calls sometimes took a
long time, while we waited patiently outside.

And, as we were no less observant than other children, we
noticed that on occasion, a nannie would come out of his private
office smiling and glowing, and scant of breath, or on another
she would emerge pale and tearful. What lay behind all this only
lucky Ailsa, worldly-wise twelve-year-old, had an inkling.

Mother, for all her gentleness of heart, would always avoid, if
possible, the presence of ugly people. She had to summon up all
her Irish courage if it became necessary to be harsh with anyone.
She surrounded herself only with attractive servants, and in
consequence we were brought up to appreciate physical beauty
as normal and ugliness as something unnatural. I am not suggest-
ing that this was a wise attitude to adopt. Looking back over the
years, I wonder whether Mr Radley realised how fortunate he
was. What an opportunity to improve his French, a little word
here and there, a little smile, a little kiss, up in the hills where
French people would usually have not been found dead, only our
young nannies, very much alive, with their warm lips; a new one
every few months, with their dark smiling eyes and he with his
bold blue ones. Small wonder he bought sweets for us!

After these visits we would return home, each time a little
more thoughtfully. But sometimes we would go to the sweet-
shop itself with Mother or with Aunt Emily, who was one of a
cluster of aunts. These arrived in monthly relays from Paddington
Station, having emerged from the, to us, mysterious squares and
crescents of South Kensington. (Once as Aunt Clara was leaving

after a lengthy visit she handed Brian, her favourite, a half-sovereign, a shining gold piece. 'You've been such a good little boy,' she said. 'Yes,' he replied, 'and I haven't once mentioned your moustache.')

It was never difficult to persuade these little old ladies that they needed more stamps, for in those days ordinary people, like the businessmen of today, were for ever writing letters. When we arrived at the village post office, there was the music of the bell as we pushed open the door, to be greeted by the brave smell of bull's-eyes, liquorice allsorts, acid drops and black-jack, penetrating the frowsty atmosphere common to all little Welsh cottages. The old, old lady, Mrs Evan Evans (probably not more than forty), popped her little hands in and out of the bottles weighing the sweets, all the while chattering in the sing-song patois of those parts. Sometimes her granddaughter, a dark-eyed child, watched us from a doorway behind the counter. No money changed hands; we saw money, indeed, only when uncles and aunts dropped half-sovereigns into our pockets.

Mother never handled money. Bills came in monthly books, for which Turner or Madame Louise were responsible. Anything that called for instant payment was settled by one of the servants – in consequence our servants had to be well paid. Cheques to dressmakers, florists and furriers were paid monthly by secretaries who followed each other in succession like prime ministers, discharging their duties faithfully: Mr Aspinall, Mr Kelly, Miss Nichols, Mr Laing, Mr Taylor.

Mr Aspinall, who died when we were still young, must have been a pleasure-loving man. He used to drive me round the Welsh villages, and the horse would know exactly where to pull in. The final stages of the homeward journey were as exciting as any boy could wish, with the gig pitching and swinging to the music of the rattling bottles and the locals leaping into the ditches as they heard our approach.

Mr Kelly was a delightful little Irishman with a goatee beard and a shaven upper lip. Most of his time was spent at Father's office, but he paid a weekly call at our home to settle the ship-wrights' and bricklayers' bills. Mr Taylor acted as financial secretary and, apart from settling certain bills, played no part in the life of the house.

Mr Laing, on the other hand, was very much part of everything that happened wherever the family was resident. He was probably one of the last of the great private secretaries, a character in his own right, with his own private income. He had lived his entire life with wealthy people who accepted him for what he was, a man cultured in literature, music and good living, skilled in the art of making his employer's life more comfortable.

Though he ate very little himself, he was intensely interested in cooking. Before dinner he would invade the kitchen, where he would perfect the dishes, seasoning, spicing and thickening the soup, or adding a dash of brandy or white wine to the sauces. He first introduced me to many of the most pleasing things in life: Russian music, the arrangement of flowers, last-minute attentions to succulent dishes. He loved beautiful china and old silver, could recognise the various periods of jade, and, though an expert at the tiresome mumbo-jumbo of wine snobbery, was also a genuine lover of wine. When he held a piece of old china, silver or jade, it was as if it had been put into his hands by its creator. He was a master of touch, taste and smell. When he was tipsy he could dance a tango he had learned to foot forth in Chile. This was a brilliant and amusing performance because he took the part of his female companion in the dance in addition to his own.

He flaunted beautiful waistcoats, which blazed in magnificent contrast to his quiet Scholte-cut suits, and his London boots were patent leather, topped with grey buckskin. He wore a flower in his button-hole and cabochon emerald and sapphire rings on his fingers. He carried with him an atmosphere of good living and the suggestion of *fougère royale*; he was the epitome of the old-fashioned dandy with all the accessories of a discreet or frustrated homosexual. It is only looking back that I realise that at some period of his life he must have descended to the cities of the plain. I can still hear his voice over the years instructing a maid: 'Remember, no strong-smelling flowers in the guests' bedrooms.'

These secretaries were served in turn by butlers, all of whom we loved. Each was a character and a delight to us. There were no unhappy serfs in our homes. The butlers ruled the parts of our houses that lay beyond the green baize doors, brass-studded with the ace of diamonds, like playing cards. There was Chun, who was Chinese; Turner the Englishman; and O'Rourke from Dublin. Turner was perhaps the most important, for he was butler in our London home. This was a house of many rooms, of massive chandeliers, of rugs lying on slippery floors and a wonderful rope-controlled hydraulic lift that Father refused to use. Turner came of a family of Norfolk parchment-makers and was originally engaged on the recommendation of Sir Derek Keppel, Master of the Royal Household. He was, therefore, very grand, being as it were only once removed from Buck House. He was rosy-cheeked, blue-eyed, portly and dignified, just as a butler should be.

At all times, on or off duty, he was soberly and correctly dressed: a short black coat and striped trousers in the morning, and a tail-coat at night. He was perfectly valeted by the second footman, James, who himself cut a fine figure in blue tail-coat with crested silver buttons and wasp-striped waistcoat.

The first footman, Charles, wore a dark alpaca coat in the morning; sometimes he played with us in Kensington Gardens. But Turner was seen outside, in the genuine open air, of which he was not fond, only on the special occasions when he oversaw the erection of a striped canopy from the front door and the laying of a red drugget across the pavement. This came under 'ceremonial', and required his personal supervision. The youngest member of the staff was a boy of about fifteen – he wore a sort of blue Eton-jacket uniform with thirty or more little round silver buttons down his front, each one touching the next. He was the handy boy who did odd jobs around the house. He wore white cotton gloves when he was on duty, and sometimes carried them on his left shoulder secured by the silver braid that formed his epaulettes.

A few years after the Second World War Mother handed me a large round leather bag. She asked me to guess what it held. I was unable to tell her, but its weight was very substantial. When she opened it there were hundreds of those silver-crested buttons, symbols of the days that are no more.

Below stairs Turner occupied a bedroom-office with bathroom, and it was here that he entertained the wine and cigar merchants on their highly profitable monthly visits. Mr Simmonds, who came weekly to wind and oil the clocks and appreciated a glass of Harvey's Bristol Cream, was another of Turner's privileged guests; but the ordinary tradesmen were looked after by a French housekeeper, Madame Louise from the Midi, a dim, shadowy woman, frail and delicate. She was kind to us, but, though we liked her, in her presence our voices would unconsciously fall to whispers.

She was a good and faithful person who loved our mother. Frugal by nature and nationality, she strove hard to keep the household expenses down, but Mother, whose ideas never flowed in the direction of economy, would totally wreck Louise's monthly budget with one single visit to Robert Jackson's or Fortnum's.

'Mais, milady,' she would say, 'la marchandise que vous achetez file trop vite.' This was the worst argument she could have put up, for Mother ordered only what she thought people would enjoy and 'rapidly consume'. Turner, too, was a prodigal spender: the bill for flowers (which Ernest Laing arranged with Japanese skill) ran into many hundreds of pounds a year.

Later, when Father became a Member of Parliament, his political secretary was Miss Nichols, but besides constituency matters she also wrote out the larger cheques. Father had a curious way of dealing with his correspondence. Letters would be put on any convenient chair or table, and, when these were covered, the rest would be scattered on the floor. He would then pace from one to the other dictating his replies. The stack of bills Miss Nichols kept on a side-table next to her typewriter. Madame Louise and Miss Nichols formed the economy party, waging bitter war each month with Turner and Mr Laing. How much Father was aware of these faction fights we never knew, but Turner had one great strategic advantage in that he was the first to see Father in the morning and the last to see him at night, and thus had the golden opportunity of getting in with the first word and driving it home with the last.

Accused by the economy party of failing to keep within her budget, because a bill for £800 had just been received from Debenham's, Mother replied haughtily: 'How dare you say that I'm not economising! Only last week I told Mr Laing to cancel the *Daily Mirror*.'

Another of her economies or compulsions was to buy any cheap dress that caught her eye. These 'bargains' justified all other extravagances. At her death they were found hanging still unworn in her wardrobe, score upon score.

The truth was that Mother had been brought up in a generation when the girls of the family were taught to play the piano, to sing, to sew, to read the major and occasionally the minor poets and the established classics, but in total innocence of the economic facts of life.

Although we were so numerous we seldom quarrelled among ourselves, and, if we did, it probably involved one of our dogs, for we moved about with packs of every breed, half-breed and quarter-breed. Most of them, like my friends in later life, were good company, but rarely well-behaved.

They occupied the most comfortable chairs, ate off our plates and slept in our bunks. Each dog had at least two friends that he would invite, and, when these strangers saw the excellent dog-meals served by our beloved cooks, they very quickly made a habit of arriving, uninvited, bringing with them, in turn, their own close friends. At one o'clock the stable-yards at Aberduna Hall and Ravenspoint were littered with so many clattering dog-bowls that even the ponies in their stalls became nervous and restless, not to mention the gardeners in the potting-sheds.

Father often complained about the ever-increasing number of dogs, but it had long been understood that he had a 'thing' about strange dogs and was always too kind-hearted to banish one, so nothing was done about it. He must have enjoyed visiting the homes of his friends, where there might be no more than four or five animals in residence. Yet he himself had no hesitation in introducing pets into the home. Once he bought Brian a stork.

It was roughly a million times the size of Nancy's canary and twice as tall as any of us. Brian was delighted with his new pet, and at the same time nervous of his responsibilities.

From the first the bird had behaved very coolly towards him, and had made it clear that it preferred its own company to his. A few evenings later Father, returning home, decided to walk from the beginning of the lane. About half a mile from the house, to his surprise, he met the stork. Being a modest man he did not flatter himself into believing the bird had ventured out in order to walk back in his company, so he attempted to drive it before him. This was not as easy as he had supposed, for the stork, having only recently left the house, had no intention of returning. It took Father the best part of the afternoon and evening to coax it even in the direction of the house.

The creature insisted on visiting every farm in the district, it flapped onto trees, climbed rocks, waded into streams, gazed thoughtfully into pigsties, and only occasionally turned round when it wished to observe what Father (faint, but pursuing) was up to. Eventually it hopped over a ten-foot ditch and was lost to sight.

That evening as usual Father told us a bed-time story, in which he rather pointedly referred to the shocks and disappointments that we would all experience in the course of life, and how we must face difficulties with a stiff upper lip, and so forth. We were then sent off to bed. Brian, however, was invited to present himself in the smoking-room after he had undressed and got into his pyjamas, to be told more and consoled for his loss. Afterwards Father went to his room, where, after taking his bath, he changed for dinner as usual. On entering the bathroom he saw the stork standing, one-legged, gazing at him with the greatest hostility from the bath-water.

The stork was eventually given away. To make up for the loss of the bird Father bought Brian a cello. This was not at all Brian's idea of a suitable substitute, as it necessitated taking lessons on the instrument. For some months he was driven to his cello lessons in the brougham, until one morning the instrument and case fell out of the window, and the rear offside wheel passed over it, with gratifying results. However, Father had by then forgotten the whole thing, so no further mention was made of it, and Brian's musical career ended to his satisfaction.

Dinner was always a ceremonious meal, candle-lit and luminous with silver, presided over by Chun at High Meadow and Aberduna, by O'Rourke at Ravenspoint, and by Turner in London. The household and guests wore black ties, the butler and footmen wore white, or vice versa. Sometimes, when there were no guests, we would be allowed down for the entrée, accompanied by a glass of white or red wine. Turner, who was never known to drop an h, invariably pronounced it 'whine', and if someone told an amusing or risqué story he would always discreetly raise his hand over his mouth to hide his smile. The length of time that we stayed up varied according to Father's mood, and sometimes we survived even to the savoury, which was always exciting – devilled something or other riding on horseback. After the fruit, which included fresh pineapple, Father liked to eat ginger out of round white pots laced in wicker nets. Once, when a new cook served rabbit, he shouted at O'Rourke in furious rage: 'In this house we never eat animals that we keep as pets.'

The signal for our departure was a slight inclination of his head. This was known as 'the bow', and to receive it was rather like catching the Speaker's eye. 'The bow' was not exactly an order; it gave you permission to withdraw, but it was regarded as slightly stronger than a hint.

One was extremely lucky to remain 'unbowed' when the grown-ups had full glasses of port and the sparkling decanter had come to rest in front of Father, and when the cigars were alight and the lovely smell of coffee was drifting about the room. In later years, when my twin brothers Ambrose and Godfrey were about ten, they would sneak down to the dining-room, finish off any wine that remained in the glasses and collect the cigar butts, of which they had a fine stock. Before we slept the aroma of Havana tobacco would creep up to our landing, and with this delicious fragrance I shall always associate Father.

Storms at Aberduna were frequent. It was there that I first

realised that I was mortally afraid of thunder and of lightning, its sinister companion, particularly frightening when it was accompanied by the smell of burned rubber. The clouds would bank up over Vindick and spill into the valley. All night the black woods would be lit in flashes and the hills would be crowned with thunder. Storms seemed to search us out as if they knew our isolation. They would encircle Vindick and crash round the house in a hollow metallic booming, which, in our imagination, echoed through the disused mine-shafts that lurked in the spinneys. Next morning the water would be high in the splash across the Marsavon road – even up to the hub of the gig's wheels.

There were sinister things about Aberduna that filled our minds with mystery. Apart from the old mine-shafts, there was the river Leet that was sucked into a mysterious underground tunnel; and sometimes at night we would hear screams from the little cottage where a black-bearded man and his woman lived on the side of Vindick. There were man-traps in the woods too, for the countryside was alive with game, and where you have game you have poachers.

With the twilight we knew that the silent marauders were moving out with their ferrets and their nets, but later we might hear that most sinister sound, the report of a single shot fired in the night by someone unknown moving cautiously in the woods. We knew every corner of our valley, every turn in the winding road, every stile and every tree that harboured nests.

Father had laid out a narrow-gauge railway at the bottom of the home wood with carriages in which we pushed each other. Sometimes in the evening we would leave the train at one end of the line, only to find it next morning at the other. No one would speak, we would avoid each other's eyes, but we all knew that in the night someone or something had been there. At Aberduna there was always a sense of imminent danger as darkness fell.

I was growing up quickly. It was already a long time since it had been fun to blow on Father's half-hunter watch and see it flick open. Exciting events were constantly taking place on the farm: a mare was in foal, a new threshing-machine arrived, haymaking started.

Mother had finished embroidering initials on my handkerchiefs, but I still had three more days of freedom. In the woods the poachers' snares would be working after I had gone, and there would be fewer birds winging their way home, and fewer animals scurrying to their burrows. I held the straight stick I always carried firmly at my side like a sword. For the next holidays Mother had promised I should have a dark fawn chamois leather jerkin with a broad leather belt and a large silver buckle like D'Artagnan's – and a white-and-scarlet scarf, for, as I was born in July, Mother had told me I could wear all the colours of the rose.

Through the slender columns of the pine-trees I could see the old disused potting-shed, a favourite retreat. I felt a sharp pang of regret that I had not been there more often; I imagined it could do more to comfort me than any human being; it could enfold me in its singing silence and smother me in the comforting acrid smell of nettles and earth and roots. The door wheezed open against a rusty spring. When it closed behind me I was in a place where I felt completely alone, where the distant cries of my brothers and sisters, playing in the woods, were like voices from another world. Then, one evening, it was different inside the hut.

I no longer heard the song of silence, throbbing like a swarm of bees in my ears. I was going to school next day, but now my eyes were dry. I pressed my stick to my side. A boy must travel to become a man. If the trees grew high at Aberduna, and the hill-tops were lost in the mist, what must the wonder of a hundred miles away be?

That morning the little girl at the post office, when she heard that I was going to school, had looked at me with grave eyes. 'Is it far away?' she had asked. 'Oh, miles and miles,' I answered, casually. I remember she had made a little surprised cry like a frightened animal and her eyes were glistening.

Impatiently, I pulled open the door of the shed. Evening was creeping up the side of Vindick and, more important than that, I had started my love-and-hate affair with life.

2

¡Señor, Salud!

MY FIRST term at my preparatory school was probably
much easier than that of most boys, because my brother
Denys had already cut the steps up the steep slope. All
I had to do was to put my feet in them and avoid slipping. The
school was in Warwickshire, a beautiful barbed-wire-less county
inhabited by a large number of florid hunting people. But I
missed the valleys and mountains of Wales.

There were many small woods, known here as spinneys, not
the wild woods we knew that sprawled and wandered over the
hills, but neat little enclosures, where foxes lived and pampered
birds were pleased to nest. There were fewer rabbits than at
home, and never the sight of an eagle; but there were plenty of
wood-pigeons winging home in the twilight.

The school was built in two styles of architecture: the new
part was Victorian-Tudor, with crude stained-glass windows,
tall and heavily mullioned, and exquisitely painted ceilings. The
older was a sort of Jane Austen–Brontë period rectory – and
plenty of it; but this was the heart of the school, while the new
was only the body. Through the old part, dark corridors
wandered as it in search of rooms with low ceilings and frowning
windows; narrow stairs appeared in unexpected places, and over
all there was the atmosphere of impending doom, for the old
house had a sombre life of its own. It was on this side that the
headmaster lived; and it was here that a boy had to grope his
way down the long, dark corridor that led to his study. This
frightening room was divided. The first half was known as the
Holy Place; from there a low Norman arch hung with a green

velvet curtain led into the mysterious second part known as the Holy of Holies.

Outside, ivy covered the old house as thick as Dorset thatch; and, curiously, where the new house joined the old, the ivy stopped abruptly. The interior of the new edifice had a permanent smell of foolscap, chalk and wax-polished floors.

The headmaster was an Old Marlburian who rather disloyally recommended parents to send their boys to Rugby. He strode the corridors and class-rooms in a black gown draped to his body like the wings of a sullen crow. He taught Latin to the higher classes, preached on Sundays, read prayers daily and invited each boy to breakfast twice a term. I managed to keep fairly successfully out of his way for three terms, but when a meeting was unavoidable he was always pleasant. On one occasion he gave me a peach, which he had surprisingly discovered, he explained, among the vegetables assembled for the harvest festival.

He never caned me, though once he should have done so had I not cheated him of the pleasure. One night the usual pillow-ragging had been going on, and though the headmaster had cat-footed into the dormitory (our school 'intelligence' being excellent) the warning signal had been received and no one was surprised out of bed. Unfortunately he had heard us and knew exactly what had been going on. Without asking us individually, he ordered those who had been out of bed to own up. This the others did, but I did not. I was full of sympathy when next morning they were caned, but I saw no reason why I should surrender myself voluntarily when I had successfully taken every precaution to avoid detection. No doubt I stamped myself among my fellows as a cad, but confession, I believed, was a matter between a man and his priest, and not between boy and master.

Punishments were often stupid and imposed for the wrong reason. At the opening class each day, boys were asked to raise their hands if they had not already paid a visit to the loo, known as the 'bogs'. On the only occasion when I confessed I had not been there I was ordered to write out one hundred times, 'Constant irregularity necessitates drastic treatment.'

School was bearable only because I treated it as an adventure. Here life was divided into two camps. As in Father's stories of the House of York and the House of Lancaster, white roses and red, it was for me to choose which colour to wear. I revelled in my friendships and chose my enemies carefully; but I was in a hurry to get on with life.

The assistant masters consisted of those who had just arrived and were just about to leave – and of those who had been there for years and were too old to find a job elsewhere. Occasionally a new one would come from Oxford or Cambridge with a half-blue: these rarely stayed for more than a term or so. They shared our badly cooked luncheons in the big hall, but they lived in rooms and studies in what was known as the 'masteries'; they ate who knows what at night in their common room, cold meat, probably, and pickles with bread and cheese. I never saw a master drink wine, nor did I ever detect the smell of beer on a master's breath, but then I was never nearer to one of them than was absolutely necessary. They were paid £150 a year. With short terms and long holidays, theirs must have been a difficult and seldom rewarding existence.

There was one master who used to lean over our desks to correct our arithmetic; at the same time he would rub his rough face against one's cheek. Fortunately he always reeked of eau-de-Cologne, and we were thus warned of his approach. He soon learned which boys liked his affectionate mannerism or were prepared to tolerate it. Those who did were invited to his study for extra tuition. I was told that there was a cupboard that held the same sweet-bottles we used to see in the village shop at Aberduna and that a boy could expect an even stronger whiff of eau-de-Cologne from his handkerchief and particularly from his carefully ironed moustache. He was probably no more than an 'old auntie', and a kind one at that, and, given the opportunity with the same possibilities, would have been equally happy teaching at a girl's school.

I was pleased when Father, at my request, asked him to stay with us on his way to Ireland, where he was to spend the holidays. I was resolved to keep the poor man's weakness a secret.

Instinctively I must have realised that Father was so essentially heterosexual that he would not have believed any other attitude was possible among those he met socially, let alone permissible. Although I had avoided the master at school I felt gratified when I saw that Mother had forgotten nothing that would add to his comfort. It was the first time that Father and Mother had entertained a guest of my chosing as opposed to family friends, and I experienced a completely new kind of warmth towards them.

I think everyone was sorry to see him leave, even though he sang songs at the pianoforte after dinner. In a sort of way he was *my* friend. Francis, the footman said: 'I don't know what kind of school you go to, Master Rupert, but at mine a master wouldn't have had holes in his shoes.' I ignored the remark because I had already learned that most chauffeurs and all manservants were snobs.

There was one master, Granville Earle, to whom I shall always be grateful, for he recounted rather than taught history. He paraded it before my dreaming eyes like a pageant. I learned history through the kings of the period, their manners, their pursuits, their battles and their mistresses; and later – under another great historian, George Townsend Warner – I was to continue rummaging in similar dust-heaps. I thus learned to distinguish between the different ages, their arts and arms, their loyalties, passions and treacheries.

At Bilton, though the library was not a good one, the books were kept on the shelves behind latticed wire like wild animals; and the cages were opened only once a day.

But here I discovered Dumas and was carried up to heaven. He may have taken grave and charming liberties with history, but his books first taught me to be interested in the story of France. I counted spiders with the mad Louis XI, rode to Paris with Henry of Navarre, threw a glove in Richelieu's face, and kissed the little hand of Louise de La Vallière. I wandered down the pages of French history as most of us have wandered down the corridors of the Louvre, Versailles and Fontainebleau.

I made two close friends at Bilton, and I believed our friendship

B

would last for a lifetime; but it was not to be like that. Freddie
Selous was the son of a great African hunter. Even at that age he
was a naturalist and entomologist and man of the woods. The
other, George Robinson, came from Winscombe in the lovely
county of Somerset. Both could tie knots, handle ferrets and
shoot catapults with unerring aim. For someone who lived in his
imagination, in palaces and castles, in dim-lit alleys of medieval
cities, they acted as a corrective. We three kept as close together
as the musketeers. We all played in the Rugger XV, though I
hated the game. I loathed the heaving, seething, battling turmoil
of the scrum with its perspiring proximity to the other players.

Cricket I loved in a masochistic way. I appreciated its orderli-
ness, the half-serious, half-humorous play on the nerves and the
green season of the game.

When our time came to move on, George came with me to
Harrow, but Freddie went four miles out of the drive to Rugby.
A few years later a bullet from an enemy plane furrowed across
Freddie's smiling eyes and sent him hurtling to his death.

In the 1914–18 war George moved on the right squares. He
bent his body to the empty air and leaned his head in the correct
direction, at the correct elevation, at the correct moment, and
consequently survived unscathed. A few weeks after he had been
demobilised, while out shooting, he climbed a stile with a loaded
gun under his arm. The ghost of a thwarted enemy must have
seized the opportunity and squeezed the trigger. Gallant George
and Smiling Freddie were great people while they lasted.

At this time none knew that the timber for the myriad crosses
that were soon to be carved was ready for the felling; so they all
worked and played as though God was to be kind to them.

On Sunday there was often a visiting priest to sermonise. The
pulpit was richly carved and dominated all, rather as the crow's-
nest in a ship commands sight of the deck as well as the horizon.
It had at least five steps leading up to it. Sometimes the sermons
were long, and I would envy a certain master his well-camouflaged
Sporting and Dramatic. I used to set next to Freddie until he
started skinning dead rabbits during the sermon. I liked the
evening hymns and the organ-music, and I believed that I was

what the English call 'musical'. I had every reason to be. On Mother's side we were of Irish descent with Hungarian blood coming from a line of impetuous men and women impatient to love and be loved. Philip Reinagle was a Royal Academician, and his gloomy landscapes are magnificently depressing. Years later, at the house of Lord Lovelace, I saw several of Reinagle's pictures: but this is the only time I have seen any outside our own collection. The story went that his brother, who was a violinist, had played one day before the King of Spain with such feeling that he burst his heart and died on the steps of the throne, to the extreme annoyance of His Catholic Majesty.

At Bilton the masters all sang for their bread and butter – and butter only because it was in the time before margarine came into general use:

> While in more lengthened notes and slow
> The deep, majestic, solemn organ blows.

The headmaster appeared to be quite indifferent to music. It was said that one Empire Day Mr Lucas, a pale, shadowy being like most organists, played 'Rule, Britannia' instead of 'God Save the King'. One of the parents remarked on this to Mr Earle. Mr Lucas, when reproached for the substitution, replied: 'Well, the organ-blower blew "Rule, Britannia", so there was nothing I could do but to play it.'

'I quite understand, and thank you for explaining,' said the headmaster.

There were half-term concerts when we saw the masters in their blue camphor-redolent serge suits. The concert hall was filled with bright-eyed mothers and well-behaved fathers. The headmaster had a word and a smile for everyone, particularly those boys who were with their parents. But it was at the regular Sunday night concerts, mediocre though the music probably was, that I first experienced the exhilaration of sound.

I took piano-lessons from Miss Sadd, who had been many years at the school. After a year she realised that she could no more teach me to read music than I could teach her to speak Chinese. Instead of making a progress-report, during my

lesson-time she would play Debussy, Ravel a nd Scriabin for
my pleasure. She knew that I loved music and that I was able
to improvise in the keys of C and B flat, though I had not the
vaguest idea why they were thus called. I was very grateful to her
then and even more so now, because music since those days has
been a comfort and a delight all my life.

It was some time before I dared ask Mother to invite her for
the holidays, and I am ashamed when I remember that it was
because she was so ugly. From being very shy at first, Miss Sadd
soon became acclimatised to our unorganised life. Mother, like
most of her generation, played the piano and sang exquisitely.
She had the great gift of being able to express herself equally
well in music and writing as in conversation. She never failed to
leave a story better than she found it.

Mother's letters would come daily, full of news and with
sometimes a piece of chocolate, a flower or a silk handkerchief.
Her style was so vivid and illuminating that she seemed to be in
the room with me when I opened her letters. She always wrote
'To' in one corner in her decisive way, as though there might be
some doubt about it. Her letters followed me all my life to many
corners of the world. When I was in France during the First
World War she used to write daily, so often that the letters
would reach me in great batches. She never lost faith in me:
cheering, comforting, overflowing with love and sympathy.
Even now an old letter is lying somewhere near me, and I feel
her presence close and her cool hands stroking my head.

Often Mother used to visit Dunchurch, the near-by village,
for weekends unbeknown to the school authorities. I used to find
my way secretly to the Dun Cow, the old coaching inn, where
she would sit writing letters, waiting the whole day to see me for
perhaps no more than an hour.

Father used to come at half-term, a tall, brown-faced man, in
perfectly fitting clothes, a soldierly figure among the shambling
masters. He used to tip those who could make life pleasanter for
me, and never forgot to look after old Bailey, organ-blower,
gardener and keeper of the lodge gates. I believe the old fellow
made straight for the Green Man, where he remained day and

night until the money was spent. But as a consequence, the lodge gates were never closed to me, and I knew well the surrounding villages, for I was already acquiring a taste for travel. There was one road, straight as one of Napoleon's and tree-lined, known as the Coventry avenue. We never penetrated far, but I could always imagine the doomed spire rising above the city at the end of the long road. I believe that even then I knew that one day the great cities of the world would be as familiar to me as the little village of Dunchurch, for already my eyes were searching the horizon.

Three times a week some of us would ride the muddy countryside on horses from a near-by hacking stables run by a rosy-faced man with the appropriate name of Gilpin, who smelt of a mixture of saddle soap and Elliman's embrocation.

Looking back it seems strange that additional food was served to boys whose parents could afford to pay for it. On birthdays boys would laboriously list those invited to take a portion of their cake, which was handed round by the totties (footmen), but on my birthday no list was necessary as it was in July and Mother would send strawberries and raspberries and cream sufficient for the whole school, including the totties, so I was spared the cruel ordeal of selection.

My parents would take a suite of the musty-smelling rooms at the Dun Cow, and here I used to entertain my friends. The extra sitting-room became a junior Fortnum & Mason's, stocked with hams, chickens, tongues, Strasbourg pâté, strawberries, raspberries, peaches, apples, bananas, cakes, pies, chocolates, sweets, *marrons glacés*, great jugs of cream fresh from the farm and manjar-blanco, a sweet concoction she had learned to love in her girlhood in Chile.

My friends loved Father: they knew he could drive a cricket ball out of any ground in England; they knew that he had broken a pavilion window at Lord's, playing for Cheshire against the M.C.C. He had played fives for Winchester and he was a first-class racquets and squash player. He smoked delicious-smelling cigars, drank port after his dinner, built ships and had a better knowledge of Greek and Latin than our classical master.

It was a great disappointment to him when my brother Denys
the dreamer, always delicate and rheumatic, was advised by
doctors that Winchester lay too low for his health and that Eton
was in the damp Thames Valley. It was decided, therefore, that
it had to be Harrow. No other school was considered, because
Father's Wykehamist attitude to the others, however splendid,
had always been 'Eton we know, and Harrow we know, but who
are ye?' I was delighted when I heard that Denys was going
there. I knew that my turn would come. I had already delved into
Byron, Trollope and Sheridan, and I, too, wanted to climb the
hill to the school for poets, writers and adventurers.

As term followed term at Bilton, it became more difficult for
me to sustain my chameleon-like existence. When I won the
swimming championship I had to appear for the presentation of
the cup, and the headmaster announced: 'The championship this
year has been won by a boy called Grayson, but the really
interesting thing is that it has been won in the slowest time in the
annals of the school.'

But it was the holidays between the school terms that had
increased in interest. Father had become enthusiastic about
motoring. Those were the days when we wore white linen coats
and goggles for the occasion, and the occasion would often be a
picnic in a Manet setting, for which Mother and my sisters wore
veils over their little straw hats, knotted beneath their chins. I can
still see their smiling lips and dancing eyes as we set off for an
afternoon in the sunshine. We had a chauffeur, a keen-eyed ex-
Naval man called Davis, with Tom Hughes as under-man for
station work. Davis was that exceptional type of driver, one who
drives fast and yet seldom uses his brakes. He persuaded Father
to buy one car after another, which was interesting and profitable
for Davis, who doubtless had an arrangement with the suppliers;
but it also delighted Father, because it always gave him an
excuse to get down to his plans for building a larger garage.

The body of our first car was shaped like a wagonette, with a
door in the rear, and the passengers sat facing each other. This
was followed by one in which the seat next to the driver slid
sideways to admit the passengers into the back, which was known

as the *tonneau*. I remember the excitement over our first car to have side-doors. It was a grey Silent Knight Minerva, and the body was described as 'torpedo'. In those days the manufacturers sold the chassis and engine only: the body was ordered separately from Hooper's, Stratstone or Mulliner. The colour was selected from the greys, blues, yellows, greens and black that came from the body-makers on little wooden panels.

Our first limousine was a thing of real beauty, jet black, enriched with yellow cane lattice. Already the cars has begun to overlap so that Father owned two or three at one time. We had in turn a Weigel, a Rover, an Argyll, a de Dion, a Mercedes-Benz, and a Fiat for station work. These were followed by a succession of Minervas and what was affectionately known as 'Mother's Daimler'.

The large Minerva had to have an extension to the crank-handle because on a cold morning it took two men to turn the engine over to start her. Then Father, to Mother's horror, decided to buy a car to drive himself. With alarming speed, as if he had been keeping it on the ice, Davis produced a two-seater Sizaire-Berwick with a long grey bonnet, buckled down with leather straps, a semi-racing job, strangely enough the sort of car that Davis himself longed to drive. It didn't take long for Davis to mesmerise Father into buying it. He never ventured forth without Davis following a few hundred yards in the rear, and for the best of reasons – there were no garages and a puncture was a major disaster. An additional tyre known as a 'stepney' had to be fixed in some mysterious way to the rim of the punctured wheel.

People had not yet learned to keep their chickens and pigs behind wire, and this was a great strain on the brakes unless you enjoyed roast chicken with grilled bacon every night. Never will I forget the exciting smell of acetylene as Davis lit the lamps at night to take us to a party. First the light flickered and sizzled in the gleaming reflectors, then steadied into a level glow that flooded the yard in a great white light, outlining the garage doors and the trees in the drive beyond like the wings and backcloth of a theatrical set.

It was exciting continually seeing new cars arrive. It never

occurred to us to wonder where the money came from to buy
them, or where the money came from for ponies, roller-skates,
hammocks, steam-engines or anything else we wanted. We only
knew that Father built and repaired ships. Unconsciously he
taught us all to be extravagant; especially Mother, whose gifts in
time and money to charitable organisations were munificent. Life
was running smoothly; everything, as they say, was glorious in
our glorious garden.

Had we been more experienced we might have sensed the lull
before the storm. For something was about to happen that was
almost to alter the current of our lives. Denys, who was now at
Harrow, discovered Shakespeare. Simultaneously, he decided
that he had been born to be a theatrical producer. His third and
most sinister discovery was the realisation that he had a whole
company of actors and enchanting actresses to hand. From
Harrow he sent me my part underlined in red, and from then on
no holidays were complete without the production of at least one
of Shakespeare's plays. At night I used to spend long hours with
a torch under the bedclothes learning my part. 'Methought I
heard a voice cry, "Sleep no more! Denys doth murder sleep." '

Father was not one to miss the opportunity of building
something. The coach-house of the old stable at High Meadow
was immediately converted into a theatre; a stage was erected
with the necessary rake complete with trap-door. A magnificent
proscenium was built with red velvet curtains drawing up into
the corners, just as they did at His Majesty's Theatre in the
Haymarket. The saddle-room became a green-room; and the
harness-room and loose boxes were divided into dressing-rooms.
Father then built an auditorium with seating for a hundred.

Denys had begun to exercise his talents, and he was determined
to develop ours. It was, no doubt, excellent training, but it was
not my idea of a holiday, and right up to the dress rehearsals I
was still learning my lines. This led to unpleasant moments
(which were quickly forgotten after a successful first night), but
Denys was a hard taskmaster, as an actor-manager, aged sixteen,
had perforce to be. At one dress rehearsal we were all very sorry
for Brian when, five minutes before the curtain-up on *Macbeth*,

he asked Denys: 'How does a second murderer brush his hair?'

During my time at Bilton I was occasionally employed in the carpenter's shop with its resinous smell of freshly sawn pine and the sweet effluvium of hot gooey glue. Mr Weston, carpenter-in-chief, whose mouth was always so full of nails and screws that it was impossible to hear what he said, failed to teach me even to use a hammer. All I really wanted was to make a cedar lining for one of mother's hanging cupboards, but it was not to be. The outcome of months of hard work was a bread-platter, not quite round, rather splintered and almost flat. It eventually made a magnificent projectile for skimming across the duck-pond at Aberduna.

I cannot remember whether the idea was to make bread-platters or to build rabbit-hutches, but the family became temporarily interested in carpentry, and Father immediately built a shop fitted with a bench and a full complement of tools, none of which any of us (including him) knew how to use. Though I had no skill, I had the ideas, and so the first thing we made was a set of wooden false teeth for Sarah MacPhillips, Mother's old sewing-maid. This dear old lady worked in a room at the far end of a long passage under the eaves, along which anyone over five feet high was obliged to stoop. The room smelt of stuffs, cottons, silks, alpaca, mixed with the faint whiff of an oil that she used for the sewing-machine. She was never happier than when telling stories about former husbands, of whom there had been five. To us she was a cross between Bluebeard and Henry VIII, as five husbands took some accounting for.

Sarah was a 'grave-gloater' with a truly gruesome mind, for husband number three had been an embalmer, and she could describe in detail a body laid out and ready to 'pass over'. We loved her description of a funeral cortège: the beautiful black hearse with its shining silver fittings, the horses' black tails sweeping the ground, the escort of sad, silk-hatted mutes.

Our favourite song from her old lips was 'The Mistletoe Bough'. It was the story of a young bride who, during a game of hide-and-seek at her wedding-party, hid herself in an old oak chest. Too late she realised that the lid was too heavy for her to lift from inside, and her bridegroom, who must have been a stupid young man, failed to find her. Centuries later her skeleton was discovered, 'gowned' in her wedding dress, which in some curious way was still white and beautiful. It was a depressing song – I have never heard it since those days, but I believe that not even Callas could have surpassed Sarah's pathetic rendering.

Sarah taught me to sew. I made dresses of striped print, blue and pink, for Miss Catchpole, who had been summoned as usual, rather optimistically, to improve my mathematics during the holidays. I learned later that Sarah at night substituted her neat stiches for my irregular ones, but Miss Catchpole must have been pleased with my summer gift, because the ruler lay idle in her long white hands for the rest of the holidays.

Numerals confused me, and to distinguish between left and right I had to feel the varying strength of my fists. My greatest worry on first going to school had been time. I was always in pursuit of it, for, as I had not then mastered the mysteries of the clock, I had to be dependent on my fellows. I hated time then as I fear it now. Would I ever be able to tell the time? Could a man go through life without knowing how to tell the time? That was the question that plagued me.

I was badly in need of coaching, I lacked concentration. Hence Miss Catchpole enjoyed her life more than a governess in those days was supposed to have any right to; for Father regarded travel as the quickest and surest way of learning, and, so that precious hours of study would not be wasted, she usually accompanied us on our journeys.

Though Father seldom made sweeping statements, I think he could have said: 'I do so love abroad.' He had followed the sea, had felt the hearts of many ships and moved to their pulsing, laughed and wept with them, known them from stem to stern. He had watched many masts drawing their circle about the sun, or pitching a line against a windy sky and following sea, or at night motionless like dreaming spires pointing to the stars. He wanted to introduce us to the joys of living (his sorrows were strictly his own), so he took us off the nursery slopes earlier than we should have left them.

The advice that Father used to give me at different times, though probably little of it original, was for me memorable. I quote as examples: never chase two hares at the same time; be wary of men who walk silently; never drink against a teetotaller; never start something that you can't finish; stretch your legs according to the length of the blanket. And I was to remember three more things: never have an affair with a woman and discuss it afterwards; always pee when you get the opportunity; and never leave the red ball over the pocket.

We sailed the Norwegian fjords as far north as the midnight sun, explored the Grecian islands, travelled the smooth waters of the Nile up to the second cataract. We sailed the hundred and sixty-five turbulent sea-miles from Ushant to Finisterre and south to Madeira. Father forbade us to be seasick, though I remember very often feeling like it. But we were not always at sea; the corridors of the Ritz-Carltons, the Grands, the Beaux-Sites, the Palaces, the Métropoles and Hermitages became our playgrounds; we learned how to skim a beer-pad from our hotel window almost up to the very feet of Napoleon standing so scornfully on the top of his column in the Place Vendôme.

The valets, hall-porters, *maîtres d'hôtel*, *femmes de chambre*, *chasseur*, were our friends ashore; at sea the bosuns, the deck-hands, the firemen.

On board ship we were forbidden to make friends with other passengers during the first week; we remained *en grande famille* or spent our time with the crew. Father had always believed in the slow approach to people. 'Never get too involved,' he would say. He disliked being addressed by a stranger, but he had no hesitation when he himself wanted to do the talking. These ideas of his annoyed us, because, like Mother, we enjoyed meeting strangers. Father enforced this rule only because he was afraid that we might get mixed up with people whom he might not like. It always made us furious, therefore, Mother included, when we had to watch him slowly getting hopelessly involved himself (usually on the boat-deck under the stars) with some woman whom he had previously warned us to avoid. Father, for all his experience of life, was no judge of men or women. He could rarely read another man's thoughts, a defect I have inherited from him.

Suddenly, I knew how to tell the time. It came to me in a delayed flash of understanding after I had been shown a sundial with the sinister warning engraved upon it: 'It is later than you think.'

However particular Father might be about punctuality, time and dates, Mother always had to remind him of our birthdays. Then one day I surprised him, before Mother had warned him of my approaching birthday. I had been reading the life of General Wolfe and had persuaded Davis to run me down in the Minerva to Westerham, the General's birthplace. Since then this market-town has acquired additional fame through Winston Churchill, who lived near by. My mind was full of Canada, so I asked Father whether he would take me there.

He asked me why, and when I explained he immediately unearthed histories and maps of the campaign. We were soon tracing Wolfe's route up the St Lawrence as he moved against Montcalm's position; together we scaled the steep Heights of Abraham, and there we refought the battle. I knew then that he was my man.

'How old are you, Rupert?' he asked suddenly.

'Fifteen,' I replied.

'I'll take you there as soon as you're sixteen.'

'That's wonderful,' I replied, 'because I'm sixteen tomorrow. Shall I pack my bag?'

He meant a thing when he said it, and he liked hurried preparations and sudden departures. We sailed on the *Empress of Ireland* with ten trunks, each striped with its bands of green, mauve and white for easy recognition. In those days people had not learned to travel light. With us there were always as many 'wanted on voyage' cabin-trunks as those that went into the hold; in addition there were numberless travelling rugs, monogrammed and of different colours.

Had Mother been travelling with us there would have been far more, as she liked to take her own bed-linen and towels wherever she went. This time she couldn't come with us, because she had a string of bazaars, sales of work and charity concerts to attend; but Ailsa and Nancy came, the fair sister and the dark one.

Father spent most of his time with the captain on the bridge, or with the Walkers, who were travelling to Vancouver. Herbert Walker was at that time General Manager of the London & South-Western Railway. Ailsa and Nancy made a slave of the Vicomte de la Chapelle, then a captain in the 60th Rifles, and of Jerry Bucknall; those two appeared to be uncertain as to which, the dark or the fair, most attracted them.

By that time I knew that all my sisters' friends were more or less in love with them, so I had learned to shift for myself. It was not long before I found a little girl-friend and because she had liked soft drinks and liqueur chocolates I had to go to Father for the first time, but not the last, for money.

I hired her a costume for the fancy-dress dance and bought her a yard of blue ribbon to encircle her waist. Among her accomplishments was that of being able to spit from her deckchair over the promenade-deck rail, but her knowledge did not extend to General Wolfe or Montcalm, even though she was Canadian-born. Was it possible that these two gallant gentlemen were not as important as I had imagined? It was with regret that I parted from her at Quebec, for her parents were taking her direct to Toronto.

We stayed at the Château Frontenac, the large hotel built in French-Scottish baronial style and mounted on the splendid Dufferin Terrace. Father was never fond of personally conducted tours. On arrival in some strange city he would leave us to settle in and go out alone to spy out the land. Later he would lead us to anything that had interested him.

We saw many of the musts – the museums, art galleries, historic buildings and so on, that every traveller sees, but he was an expert in collecting vignettes, an interesting house, a river view, a café, a forgotten square. He was continually pointing out things that still live in my memory.

Father spoke very little French, but he had a knowledge of the written word. In Quebec he insisted on my speaking French, but

I found the Canadian French spoken there difficult to understand. On one occasion I happened to refer to a *double entendre* and he said: 'I understand what you wish to imply, but there is no such expression as *double entendre* in French. You mean *à double entente*.' And he was quite right. He even knew the feminine of *lièvre*.

One day we visited the Montmorency Falls; on another we crossed downriver to Rimouski on the south bank. We were taken there on a shipowner's yacht and generously entertained: he wanted Father to buy his shipyard. Though there was great activity in the yard, to the man's obvious disappointment Father decided not to buy it. He told us later that when he had visited the place alone on the previous day there had been no work in progress. The idea of the man faking the activity settled the matter with Father. It was at Rimouski that he put his hand on my shoulder and said: 'Canada is a country for the young. There's no place for the old.'

As he spoke two of the oldest men it was possible to imagine tottered onto the quayside. One must have been ninety and the other, obviously his younger brother, was about eighty.

'That's the way it goes,' Father said wryly. 'Life's full of contradictions.'

Next day we took a river-steamer up the St Lawrence. We visited the Heights of Abraham and explored the battlefield: but all the time I was impatient and anxious to reach the Ritz-Carlton in Montreal, where I hoped a letter might be awaiting me. I was not disappointed. It was my first love-letter and one to treasure, but I never replied, because already life was moving too fast for letters.

We had been a fortnight in Montreal when Father suddenly became anxious about his 'box of bricks.' At that time he was building Ravenspoint – a new home, on a wild piece of Anglesey coastline. He must live on an island and have the sea at his door and mountains in the distance. He wanted rock for his house and river-sand for the mortar, the sea to fill the baths, and the sun to flood the windows. The house was designed and built from day to day: Father's pet architect stayed in Holyhead, alert to alter his designs at a moment's notice. Wings were erected, altered, added to: Father was digging deep into his 'box of bricks'. Mother's impetuous visits to the headland to supervise the kitchen arrangements, servants' quarters, linen-cupboards, resulted in further cancellations, alterations and additions. A road had been cut through the heather to reach the site.

Already a stone-flagged courtyard had spread itself before the front door, close-fitting as a carpet. In front of the house, which was long and low and white, a terrace stretched like the promenade-deck of a liner, a loggia with long plate-glass windows looked across the Irish Sea, and far beyond that the Atlantic. The house faced south, and the west wing, which included the breakfast-room, gun-room, playroom, kitchens, larders, etc., sprawled away in a maze of roofs and windows. Cottages were going up to house additional guests, a garage for ten cars, and alongside it an open fives-court.

Great stone walls had begun to reach out over the cliffs, twisting and turning, climbing and falling to the contours of the headland. It was to all this that Father was so suddenly in a hurry to return.

On our last night in Montreal, Juan, son of a prominent Mexican politician asked me up to his suite. At the time I had wondered why I had been invited, and it was many years later before I learned the answer. Juan was dark and handsome and a little sinister. There were two girls that evening in his sitting-room, one a Canadian (whose face I cannot recall, except that she was as fair as Juan was dark) and the other was a young Mexican.

She was curled up cat-like in a pink damask chair with her legs tucked under her, and she was playing a mouth-organ. For a moment she stopped and lowered the instrument. She looked me straight in the eyes, but there was no smile on her lips. Then I felt rather than watched the dark eyes gazing lazily over me. The blood burned in my cheeks.

After that she hardly glanced at me at all, so that I was able to watch her without embarrassment. Her face was oval, a short straight nose, black hair coming to a peak over her forehead, and her mouth, when I could see it, was the colour of a dark carnation against her honey-coloured skin.

Juan handed me a brimming glass. I drank it down, and it pierced my body like forked lightning, while the tears came to my eyes. I turned away to hide my shock. When I looked back the chair was empty. From the next room I could hear the sound of her silly music. I was sorry she had gone, for the drink now had made me feel warm and confident, and I wanted to talk to her. Then the all-wise Juan suggested that her music was calling for me.

I opened the door to the bedroom. Then I stood motionless with surprise. The girl lay naked on the bed, matt-brown against the white sheets. I realised that I had entered the room rather abruptly and had maybe taken her by surprise; so, with averted gaze, I walked to the window and stood looking down into the hotel patio.

People were seated at supper, under red-and-white striped umbrellas that sprouted like mushrooms from the tables; and there was the gleam of silver, and I could smell Cuban tobacco. I could only see the orchestra playing: their distant music was lost in the sound of the girl's mouth-organ from the bed behind me. Trembling with mysterious emotions, I stood watching the scene below. Behind me I was only too aware that a girl lay naked on a bed playing a ridiculous melody on a ridiculous instrument.

Suddenly the music stopped. Then I was impelled to turn, and for the first time she smiled, and her impassive face was lit with an expression of interest: she was like a wide-eyed, watching child. Then she began playing her silly tune again; but now her free hand drew me towards her, guiding my kisses until the music faded with a discord and her arms stole round my neck and held me tightly like a child, as though afraid that I might run away.

In the years to come I was to realise that she was one of the whore-children who drift in and out of men's lives, surprising them in their unguarded hours. Then I knew nothing of her but the exquisite pleasure of her skilled embrace.

Back in my room in the early hours of the morning, I called down to the night-desk to order dark-red carnations (on Father's account) to be sent up to the suite from one nameless to the other nameless. Then I hurled my clothes in every direction and kicked the waste-paper basket sailing through the open window. I flung myself on the bed, still redolent of her body's scent. I was never to forget this first experience of animal love, my initiation into its mysteries by a nameless, lovely, garlic-scented Mexican.

Unwittingly she had aroused in me the strange fascination of holding in my arms one of those transient girls of whose very existence I had, until that moment, been unaware.

Many, many years later, when I was drinking tequila with a bunch of bums in a bar in Mexico City, I learned that Juan, at the time I met him in Montreal, was already well known as a voyeur. Even the knowledge that I was only providing entertainment for him has done nothing to dim the glory of that first of all first nights: 'Alive or dead, across the years: ¡Señor, Salud!'

3

Halcyon Days

IN THE summers of those years before 1914 one of the great
social events and the last of the London Season was the Eton
and Harrow cricket match at Lord's. Father would hire a
coach and Turner would organise the luncheon, which was
laid out on a table alongside. The salmon and the lobster, the
strawberries and raspberries were at their prime. Another table
served as a bar, where Turner, assisted by two footmen who
flitted about his portly person like acolytes in attendance on their
bishop, dispensed champagne-cup and lemonade.

It was the season of my life, when the world seemed peopled
with lovely girls with laughing eyes under wide-brimmed straw
hats decorated with shimmering satin bows. They wore white
muslin frocks with pink, blue or mauve sashes round their waists,
and long white gloves, and as they moved about they filled the
English air with the mildly intoxicating scent of fresh sweet-peas.
Their cheeks were perfumed like peaches, and not one of them
had the faintest taint of garlic on her lips.

It was a cricket match entirely surrounded by a garden party.
It was an American woman who asked: 'What are the little boys
in white doing on the green?'

Father, as a Wykehamist, never wore a button-hole. The rest
of us loyally sported cornflowers. A constant stream of friends,
Harrovians and Etonians, past and present, called at the coach.
There was always too, a beautiful garden to visit through the
only private entrance to the ground. Here, as the guests of my
cousin Billie Findlay (who was Secretary of the M.C.C.) and
his charming wife, we met all the great cricketers, both active

and retired, at what was a garden party within the garden party.

At one match a quiet, elderly man joined us for luncheon. He spent most of the first day with us, but none knew who he was, nor did anyone care to ask him. Even Mother, who was marvellous at learning about people, was unable to find any point of contact. It was quite impossible to get anything out of him. He was wearing neither a Harrow cornflower nor an Eton carnation. He took no interest in the cricket; and Turner reported that there were no initials in the lining of his grey top-hat. He was polite when addressed, but talked very little and made no remark that could be described as personal. On the Saturday someone in our party seemed vaguely to know him, for he had again turned up for luncheon, but, unfortunately could not recall his name and remembered only one thing about him.

It seems that our stranger had dreamed about a woman he knew only casually, but his dream was so delightful and so vivid that next morning he knew that he was in love with her. That very day he chanced to meet her, proposed, was accepted and they had lived most happily since then. On hearing this charming story our regret was that he had not brought her with him. When he left he thanked Mother for the enjoyable time he had spent with us, remarking that as a child he had never liked long walks and that it was years since he had seen a cricket match.

If I had not shown much interest in our mysterious guest it was because I had been more pleasurably occupied talking to a dark-eyed girl who had just joined our party. I watched the cool shadow cast by the lace-edged parasol she was carrying, it deepened the brown of her eyes while the stippled haze of the filtered sunshine flickered and danced like sequins on her lips and cheek and hair. It was as if I had stepped out of the shimmering heat into the coloured air of a cool, lilac-scented drawing-room with its saffron light and glint of ivory. This was all hers, a special place to share with special friends, for I knew that I was only one of many, but I was young in a world that was very young and there were gardens that led to other gardens blazing with flowers, and it was no time to dally.

Sometimes we stayed to watch what *The Times* usually described

as 'unruly behaviour' at the end of the match, when people
flocked in front of the pavilion to call the sides out onto the
balconies. A friendly fight invariably developed between the
separate supporters, when the object was to bash as many of your
opponents' top-hats as came within range of the pale blue or
dark blue tasselled sticks. I remember seeing two really old men
red in the face with frustration when their umbrella handles
became interlocked and neither was able to get at the other's hat.

After the match our party would go to the Gaiety Theatre to
see the current musical-comedy, and later we would sup at
Ranelagh or Hurlingham at a cornflower-and-smilax-festooned
table, later to dance to the dreamy waltzes of Joyce, Davson and
de Zulueta. That night the West End would be crowded with
Etonians and Harrovians in white ties and tail-coats and white
kid gloves, sporting cornflowers and carnations and filling the
theatres and restaurants, while the streets and squares echoed the
long roar of 'Har . . . row', competing with the short clipped
cries of 'Eee . . . ton'.

So we played, flirted and danced. We were young in a world
that was gently sliding into the abyss, a world where the standard
of comfort for the privileged few within the citadel had never in
the history of the universe been surpassed, served and waited
upon by a further select few of the hordes who stood outside the
gates. We wore life as a suit of clothes, which, once donned,
could be forgotten. I knew nothing of poverty, frustration and
famine, and was only aware of the hot sweet smell of the flowers
in the window-boxes as I arrived home that night and handed
my white kid gloves and top-hat to one of the sleepy footmen.

I had gone to Harrow after leaving Bilton, but strangely few
memories of my school-days there stir my mind, though to most
men it is a time of intense recollection. I remember hardly any
masters, and, apart from Alex, only a few boys among them
Francis Queensberry, L. P. Hartley, Sackie McCorquodale, Peter
Hoare and Gulbenkian. Nubar even at that early age was a
character; years later, when I was dining with him at the Ritz
with his lovely second wife, he told me how the master of the
hunt he followed one day remarked that he had never seen a man

following hounds so unconventionally dressed, even to an orchid. To which Nubar had replied: 'And to me, sir, it is quite obvious, that you have never before seen an Armenian Jew in the hunting field.' Is it possible that for a large part of my time I was among some six hundred faceless strangers? Denys, before me, had distinguished himself there. Brian and Tristram were to follow and to excel at work and play, as was Ronnie Grayson, my nephew and the present head of the family, in a later generation. I was the pedestrian among the runners. Father did little to encourage me to work. He paid no attention to school reports and was interested only in that final item which came under the rather forbidding heading of 'General Conduct'.

If we were abroad with him he would be unaware that we were exceeding our allotted holiday and was quite indifferent to our reception on arrival back so late in term. He was all for learning and strongly in favour of teaching, but as a good Christian may be anticlerical, Father was anti-tutorial. Hence my own rebelliousness.

Mother, for all her Irish casualness, took a much more practical view of our studies. It was, of course, long before the days of the G.C.E. and of 'O' and 'A' levels. I believe that those of my brothers who went to Cambridge did their 'Little-Go' long after they went up. On looking back it seems that Father, bless him, was more interested in teaching us the art of living than the acquisition of knowledge from doctor or saint.

Father showed little interest when the time came for me to go to Harrow, and it was Mother who helped me to move in. It had been arranged for me to go to George Townsend Warner's, where Denys had been Head of the House. This was conveniently situated in the High Street, within easy distance of the form-rooms where we studied. I had a room on the third floor back. The only piece of furniture supplied by the House was the bed, which folded upwards into a cupboard. Mother had the room immediately repapered, and then furnished it in her usual good taste: two comfortable armchairs and a mahogany sofa-table. She insisted on a close-fitted carpet, then regarded as a luxury. Shelves were built by a local carpenter and she sent me yards of richly tooled leather for the book-case as a dust-protector. I hung my pictures, mostly drawings by Arthur Rackham and Edmund Dulac.

My chintz-framed window opened on to a fire-escape, a convenient balcony where I was able to sit on sunny days. On one side I could see Harrow church, on the peak of the hill; straight ahead I looked over miles of green well-remembered fields. The stretch of country was known by the locals as the Uxbridge Flats, and in the evening I could see the lights coming on in what was then only a small market-town.

I was, fortunately, tall enough to be allowed to wear a tail-coat, so Father sent me to be fitted at his tailor, Lesley & Roberts. 'Tails' and a Harrow straw were then the regulation kit for attending 'schools'. My 'bluer', school-blazer, worn in the afternoon, was made by Thomas Smith in the High Street.

Thus conventionally coated and comfortably housed, I began my very undistinguished career as an Harrovian. I found nothing unreasonable about the hours. They allowed me ample time for reading. I soon found my way to the Vaughan Library, which from that time became my hide-away. After the confinement of a private school I was filled with a delightful sense of freedom. I could be alone when I wished and, within the limits of the school curriculum, I could lead my own life.

The first friend I made was William Sigismund Alexander. At Harrow we knew him as Alex; but in the years ahead, in the Irish Guards, he was known as 'Baby' because he was blessed with an elder brother, Harold Alexander, later the Field-Marshal. He was in the Headmaster's House, but this made little difference, as we met daily. He had a delightful sense of the ridiculous and sharp wit, enhanced by his manner of speech, clear-cut and clipped. Had he been an opera-singer he would have been a tenor. Our mutual friend was a boy called Masterman, who with little effort became Head of the school.

I cannot say I disliked the three years I spent at Harrow, nor can I say it was a memorable time or one of abrupt awakening. Now I wonder whether the masters fared as well. If one of them was ten minutes late the form automatically dispersed.

When this happened the wretched man was probably in trouble with the authorities. Once I overhead a conversation in front of the school chapel, a constant mumbling and grumbling, interrupted at frequent intervals by a nervous voice repeating, 'Yes, Headmaster. Yes, Headmaster.'

The only bullying I ever noticed was the persecution of certain masters, particularly the inexperienced and short-sighted ones. In one form a boy regularly brought in two bricks with him. In the middle of the class he threw one brick through the window and the other at the master's desk. This skilled simultaneity gave the impression that the brick crashing against the desk had been chucked through the now shattered window. Pandemonium followed and the entire form raced in glee from the room in pursuit of the culprit. These tricks were constantly played on those masters unable to enforce discipline. No one is quicker to detect weakness in a master than a schoolboy. The life of a master, underpaid and overworked, in those days must have been misery, except for the disciplinarians and those for whom teaching was a true vocation.

For French lessons I went up to M. Prior, a totally delightful, witty man, smartly bearded. Not only was he an excellent French master, but he even looked and smelt like one.

He told me a story about Dumas *père*. A young American girl, overwhelmed on meeting the great writer, started saying: 'M. Dumas, votre nom bril . . .' Dumas at this point interrupted her: 'Young lady,' he said, 'do not go into ecstasies over something you have never seen.' The poor girl was about to say 'nom brillant'. 'Nombril', however, is 'navel'.

We had to laugh in form one day when a boy remarked: 'I'm quite prepared to pronounce these French words as you suggest I should, monsieur, but it all sounds very affected to me.'

The forms were big, too big; and often the master would be too far away to be heard distinctly. A master once asked a question (geographical, I believe) to which no one seemed to have the reply. From my end of the form room we had not even heard it. The master began pointing to each one of us in turn, seeming to say 'D'you know, d'you know', until he finally, having forgotten his original question, ended up to my surprise by answering the question himself: 'Juno, you should all know, was, of course, Juno the queen of the gods.'

One day, through pure carelessness, I was discovered using a crib (as an aid to learning) during a Latin lesson. I was duly to be sent up the Headmaster, Lionel Ford. When the fatal day came I was to wait in a sitting-room next to his study. Here I was joined by his sons, then aged six and seven. This made a pleasant distraction during a most unpleasant period, usually spent in contemplation of what was awaiting in the next room.

Many years later Lionel Ford told me that on opening the door to call me in he saw me on my hands and knees with one of his children riding cowboy on my back. He confessed that, excellent cricketer and racquets player though he was, this preview of my bottom had put him off his stroke, and he never remembered thrashing anyone with less enthusiasm.

In our second year Alex, Masterman and I decided to publish a periodical. We named it '*A la Carte*' and it was sold at the booksellers and stationers at sixpence, sale or return. It comprised an editorial, for which Masterman was responsible; local news, reported by me; and a humorous article, which naturally fell to Alex.

In the course of time the editorial became too pointed, the reporting too trenchant and the humour too satirical. We published as the spirit moved us, we sold out every issue, but gradually we fell out of favour with the establishment – the 'Bloods', all members of the Philathletic Club, the Harrow equivalent of 'Pop' at Eton. The fact that we were junior members of the school weighed against us. All might have been well, but, rather foolishly, we had begun sniping at the school authorities themselves. *The Harrovian,* the official school magazine, made a scathing attack on us. We knew that our days were numbered.

One of our issues had contained the story of a boy who had been caught returning over the roof-tops to his rooms. The boy's House was situated next to the home of a pastry cook, who not only made the best cakes in the High Street, but who was also the father of a most beguiling girl. Though the authorities had probably at first taken a serious view of this Casanovian escapade, curiously no punishment had been meted out to the offender. We drew attention to the fact that the offence had been hushed up. This was not very sporting of us, but we were running a paper and to us news and, particularly, comment was important. We were now able to disclose to our readers the reason. No proceedings had been taken against the culprit because he was a 'French boy', and thus we recorded an act of racial discrimination which to us seemed wholly admirable.

It has often been said that the public school education is conducted in an atmosphere unnaturally monastic. I was not one to develop a crush on another boy, nor did I experience any sexual interest in them. This may have been because I was early initiated in the normal relationship between the sexes. I am certain that it is ridiculous to assume that public schools breed homosexuality. At any time at Harrow there were pretty boys who were known as house-tarts; they attracted the older boys not because they were of the same sex, but because they represented the nearest equivalent to the female.

Years later, when I went to sea, it was a common thing to hear old sailors addressing each other as 'darling' and 'love'. In any community of one sex, whether adolescent or adult, tenderness invariably develops between individuals.

Exposing the authorities to ridicule in *A la Carte* was *lèse-majesté* and we were officially warned to be more careful in the future. Unfortunately the warning went unheeded, and our next issue contained a critical study of the whole public school system. We suggested that it existed for the express purpose of shielding us from our own lamentable ignorance. We accused the system of pouring us into similar moulds. Were we not taught to make games a religion and encouraged to regard the 'team-spirit' as the pattern of life? Most afternoons we were expected to tramp down the hill to the playing-fields, in step with Jesus, to the sound of a heavenly choir singing 'Forty Years On'. That, of course, was the last number to appear. The axe fell.

As Alex remarked, perhaps it was just as well, because we could now proceed with our education, adding shrewdly: 'But I still believe that "they" are more interested in schooling than in teaching.'

I entirely lacked the competitive spirit, nor was I particularly interested in acquiring the team-spirit, so there was obviously no future for me as a sportsman, though I enjoyed cricket, as I had at Bilton. In the field I stood in trembling anticipation of a catch coming towards me. At the wicket I stood shaking in my flannels as some fast bowler hurled balls at my leg-stump. It was never a surprise when the ball slipped through my hands or my stumps went flying. But the game still exercised its terrifying fascination over me.

I disliked football, particularly Harrow football, played with a ball that appeared to be almost square in shape, on the heaviest clay in Middlesex. I hated the sweating nearness of other players. In life's contrary way, I excelled at this most disagreeable game, and I was soon awarded my 'fez'.

Thus dignified I was no longer forced to play in the House games I loathed so much. Let the others knock their heads together for an hour. I took good advantage of this privilege and was seen on the football field only when a match was being played, an absence that did nothing to increase my popularity with either boys or masters.

Apart from squash racquets, my dislike for games generally increased as I grew older, and this would be regarded by most people as a weakness. It is strange how often some characteristic quality acquired at school will develop during a man's lifetime. I remember a highly emotional boy at Harrow who, for no important reason that one could see, was constantly breaking into tears. Later in life, as a bachelor he went to live with his widowed sister. One day she said to him: 'Cuthbert, you really must pull yourself together. Two mornings and you haven't finished your cornflakes, now you're crying again. Control yourself, Cuthbert; and all because you've reached retirement age.'

Like Cuthbert I had a weakness, and I believe it was that I never wished to excel. It might be suggested that had I been keener on sport I would have enjoyed them. 'I don't know,' as the Prince of Wales said when he was asked if he knew how to use a parachute, 'and I don't want to know.'

There were many things about Harrow that I loved, and I shall always be proud to have been there and grateful to Father for having sent me. On the steep lane that leads to the church-yard that crowns the hill there is an inscription on the old wall of the fourth form which reads: 'Near this spot Anthony Ashley Cooper, afterwards 7th Earl of Shaftesbury, while yet a boy in Harrow School, saw, with shame and indignation, a pauper's funeral, which helped to awaken his lifelong devotion to the service of the poor and the oppressed.'

There were many things to be learned at Harrow that were not necessarily taught in the form-rooms, the chapel or even the Vaughan Library, and the first to remember of these was that kindness and consideration to those less fortunate than oneself must be guiding principle in a civilised life.

I had many friends among the townsfolk on the hill: Willie Chatham the bootmaker, Mr Shepherd of Thomas Smith the tailor's with his assistant Mr Fewtral, and Mr Guppy of the music shop, all of whom I had accounts with. There were two dear old ladies, the Dames Armstrong, and when one of the sisters died the other described her death to Brian: 'And just before her passing she raised her little hand as if to say Cheerio!'

Sometimes during my hard-won anti-social hours I would climb alone to the peak of the hill from which the spire of the parish church arose in domination of the surrounding lands. It was the church's old graveyard that Byron, my admired and non-coeval schoolfellow – whose tastes, but not, alas, talents, I was so enthusiastically to share – had wished that he might be buried. During his school-days it was said that he would often lie on the old gravestone carved with name of one 'Peachy', long-deceased, and known to succeeding generations of Har-rovians as 'The Peachy Stone'.

Here the hill shelves sharply to the fields where Byron played cricket. Beyond the green of the meadow lies the Thames and through summer haze an occasional glimpse of Windsor Castle.

Lying stretched on the stone I could feel, as it were, some of his romantic spirit rub off on me and strove to see with his romantic eyes the selfsame scene that he had looked upon: but his flesh must have been far tougher than mine, for the Peachy stone had a most distracting lack of comfort. None the less I too was a poet.

> A shabby fellow true but a poet still
> And duly seated on the Olympian hill.

I had written a poem to the memory of Robert Falcon Scott, the Antarctic explorer; it was moreover published in *The Harrovian*. This raised me in the esteem of my Housemaster, George Townsend Warner, and from then on he befriended me, particularly when he learned of my unquenchable thirst for history, on which he was a distinguished authority. History, poetry and music enraptured me.

Father's interest in music was confined almost exclusively to Neapolitan and Sicilian songs. Mother, like most of her generation, played the piano, especially the works of Mendelssohn, Heller and Chaminade. But it was typical of Father that he should have allowed me to join the select few who were taken up to London by Percy Buck, the Harrow music master, to hear the operas at Covent Garden. I will never forget my raptures at first hearing *Parsifal*. I enjoyed, too, the dinner at the Waldorf Hotel during the long interval. My love for all types of music was seeded during these years and has remained a joy and a comfort to me throughout my life.

Two memories are painted in my mind with the clarity of a Canaletto. The first was at Covent Garden, at the first performance in London of *Il Trittico*. The curtains closed on the final notes of *Gianni Schicchi* and the applause crashed out. Suddenly, a hush fell over the opera house as the curtains parted again to reveal the small, unsmiling figure of Puccini. The entire audience rose to its feet and a storm of cheers broke like thunder. It was as if the pent-up feelings of a generation of opera-lovers had burst, like the floodgates of a great river, in gratitude to the composer of *Madame Butterfly, La Bohème, Tosca* and *Manon Lescaut.*

The second great occasion was a concert of Delius's music at the old Queen's Hall. The ovation that we gave the composer as he was gently piloted into his seat in the front seat of the circle was only exceeded by the applause at the end of the concert, when my head was reeling and my heart brimming with the beauty of *Koanga, Brigg Fair, A Village Romeo and Juliet.* Slowly the old man rose from his seat, wiping his blind eyes and bowing into his own darkness.

Mother's letters came almost daily. Father had been captaining, and no doubt financing, a cricket side on a tour in Holland. She wrote that during a particularly hilarious evening two members of the eleven had stolen a pair of his cricket boots and hoisted them up the flagpole of the hotel. All might have been well but for the fact that the following day happened to be the Queen of Holland's birthday. To the consternation and anger of the manager, the boots had become so firmly entangled in the tackle at the truck that it was impossible to get them loose. Father, always correct in matters of protocol, hurried to the British Embassy to offer an explanation and make apologies: eventually the boots were cut down, the Dutch flag hoisted and a birthday greeting dispatched to the Queen. Mother ended her letter: 'Your Father, I gather, was not amused.'

In another letter she wrote telling me about the artificial lake that Father had made for us at High Meadow. It had a small island with a rustic bridge leading to it, and a dinghy floating on the water with its own boathouse.

Father seldom visited me at Harrow: the family felt that he had not quite forgiven himself for not sending us to Winchester. But Mother came often. As at the Dun Cow at Dunchurch, she turned her rooms at the Queen's Head into a store-house of good food and the latest books, so that when I visited her with friends on Sundays it was difficult to find space for our shining top-hats. Any room she occupied, even for a short time, she made particularly her own, even to her little monogrammed vicuña shawls. Family photographs were everywhere, writing pads, stamps, masses of flowers and her own linen sheets on the beds. She had her own prie-dieu, and the windows were wide open even when it was blowing a gale. Over all was the academic smell of freshly sharpened cedar pencils.

It was after one of the Eton and Harrow matches that I first experienced the sensation of being drunk. It was to the music of bells, the jingle of harness and the clip-clop of hooves on the hard road, because I was driving home in a hansom cab at the time and the horse seemed to me to have taken wings. When the cabbie opened his little window on the roof and spoke to me I thought the floor of the cab had opened and that the end had come.

This was not to be the last alarming episode in my life, but it was one of the first, and the memory of the first of anything is something one remembers, even if one doesn't cherish it.

4

Soldier Boys

At the age of seventeen Father had been left a thousand pounds a year by his mother. He was thus agreeably independent from an early age, and this was probably the reason why, throughout his life, he preferred the more selfish role of host to the more exacting one of guest. For all his experience of life, he was no judge of men or women, except when he married my mother. The men he backed in business invariably failed. It was a strange thing that a man with so little judgement should have been able to increase a family business so successfully. He seemed always to be closer in sympathy than in understanding with those he employed, though when he wished he could impose his authority firmly and swiftly. He was amused rather than annoyed when, on reprimanding a secretary for continually being half an hour late, the man replied: 'Yes, sir, but you forget that I always leave half an hour early.'

According to the annals of Liverpool the first Grayson started building ships in 1697 at a wharf now built over and known as Grayson Street. From that time on the business passed from father to son until the death of my brother Sir Denys Grayson in 1955.

None of them were of particular interest to me, with the exception of Edward, my great-great-grandfather. This rather idealistic man, in the year 1804, became engaged in an angry correspondence with a young army officer named Sparling on the delicate ground that he had broken off his engagement to my ancestor's niece, Anne Renshaw, for no sufficient reason.

Having publicly called Sparling 'a scoundrel and a villain', Edward received a challenge, and a meeting was fixed for the morning of Sunday, 26 February 1804, opposite the ancient chapel in Toxteth Park, Liverpool. From this rendezvous the combatants and their seconds went down to the little valley known as the Dingle. Sparling's second was Captain Colquitt of the Royal Navy, and Edward Grayson's was Dr Macartney, a noted anatomist. There was a single exchange of shots, and Edward fell mortally wounded. Sparling and his second surrendered themselves, and they were tried on a murder charge at the Lancaster Assizes. Sparling happened to be a close friend of the Prince of Wales, and this may have influenced the jury, which brought in a verdict of 'Not Guilty'. Edward must have been one of the last men to be killed in a duel in England.

On my mother's side of the family we were all very proud of Daniel Harrington. who served with Nelson in the *Victory*. My uncle, Edmund Harrington, showed me his diary in which the sailor had written: 'And I can safely say that there isn't a man on board this ship that wouldn't gladly have laid down his life for Lord Nelson.'

On the opposite page was a list of clothes that he had sent to a laundry in Portsmouth and the date when he had last written to his wife. In spite of all the battles in which he had fought, he remained a lieutenant. In those days promotion went by patronage, and there was little chance of advancement for an impecunious Irishman. In his old age his cause was brought to the notice of Queen Victoria by Sir Robert Arbuthnot. Queen Victoria wrote on the petition: 'This case merits consideration.'

Lord Nelson had written a testimonial ceremonially signed and, after Daniel's death, much treasured. Her widow showed it to Lady Nelson. It was crumpled by that time, so she took it from my ancestress and gummed it onto a lace handkerchief. When I saw this a century later the paper was yellow and the ink faded, but it was perfectly legible; and so was Nelson's signature.

Nelson once said to him: 'Mr Harrington, you're getting very bald.' Daniel, who was not an Irishman for nothing, replied:

'Is that to be wondered at, my Lord, considering all the men who have passed over me.'

Father's own humour was often mildly spiced with cruelty. On one occasion he was entertaining Prince and Princess Arthur of Connaught at an hotel in Oslo. Before his guests arrived he turned to my twin brothers, Ambrose and Godfrey, then aged ten. 'I've come out without my wallet. Have either of you got any money?' he enquired with a long face. 'I don't know how we are going to pay the bill. . . . Please turn out your pockets.'

Everything came out onto the table – knives, cigarette-ends, bits of string, even a ten-Kroner note sticking to a piece of toffee.

'If that's the best you can do, perhaps we'd better give ourselves up to the police.' Father played his part so well that by this time the twins were genuinely alarmed. Fortunately at that moment the guests arrived, and the schoolboy miscellany had to be hastily concealed.

Staying with us once was an old cousin, Maude Valérie White, a famous song-composer of that period. Some of her songs, particularly Byron's 'So we'll go no more a-roving', 'King Charles' and 'The Devout Lover', are still broadcast. She had a brilliant mind, but, alas, she was huge as a mountain. Father wished to register his disapproval because she had come for a weekend and had stayed three months; so when he heard that she was dining in her room, he enquired, blandly: 'Has no one been up to see Mont Blanc to day?'

He could appreciate a joke against himself. When a friend of mine wanted him to advance five hundred pounds, he asked for one good reason why he should do so. My friend replied: 'You may decide not to, sir, but you can't say truthfully, like most men I know, that you haven't got it.' He was given the 'monkey'.

Another time, just to do a man a favour, he advanced a thousand pounds; but the recipient insisted on giving him a wad of shares in exchange. The company, it transpired, owned a cinema in the East End of London. This flea-pit had a faithful following and practically no overhead expenses. In consequence my Father said it had been one of the best investments he had

C

ever made. The L.C.C. eventually stepped in and condemmed the building.

Father's reception of people in financial trouble was very different from that of another very rich man I knew who was approached for a loan. 'Of course, I'll advance you the money,' he said, 'as much as you want, on one condition.' The borrower immediately indicated that there was no condition to which he was not prepared to agree. 'Well,' the man said 'my condition is that you tell me the name of anyone I've ever lent money to.'

Father pretended to be angry when, in August 1914, I terminated my undistinguished career at Harrow and enlisted. It was not so much that I had deserted the family and joined the King's Liverpool Regiment as a 'ranker' (though I was under age), but because I had not been commissioned as an officer through the proper channels. He liked things done in a proper and tidy way. To him it was all prefectly simple. A gentleman became an officer, and, having done so, the officer was expected to behave like a gentleman. A gentleman was a ranker only if he was an eccentric or, worse still, had something in his past life to hide.

Father took action, and when he moved he moved quickly. He went immediately to Lord Derby, who had been a colonel in the Grenadier Guards and was also a close friend of Colonel Proby, Lieuntenant-Colonel of the Irish Guards. Peers were men of influence in those days, and the following week I was summoned to the regimental orderly room, where it was agreed that I should join the regiment after I had passed out of Sandhurst.

This was not done as easily as Father imagined, for I had first to pass into Sandhurst. I was immediately dispatched to a highly successful military crammer named Malden, in the Tunbridge Wells district. He had a most delightful family of girls – which every crammer should have. The youngest of these taught me to smoke a pipe, something I had never done before, and for which I am still most grateful to her.

Until my arrival and departure it had been Mr Malden's boast that none of his boys had ever failed to pass into Sandhurst. My mathematics (an important section of the Royal Military College examination) were and had always been deplorable, and when I eventually sat for the examination at Burlington House, the majority of questions were quite incomprehensible to me.

It was here that I first met Pingo Langrishe. Neither of us wanted to go to the Royal Military College. We were interested only in getting to France before the fighting was over. At the examinations we sat out the minimum requisite time, a quarter of an hour per paper, then went across the street to the Burlington Bar. Pingo had left Eton at the same time as I had left Harrow, and we became close friends from that moment.

Having failed the exam, in due course we both joined the Irish Guards at Warley Barracks with direct commissions, and no gentleman-cadet nonsense. Here the light and laughter in the life of a young ensign was continually threatened by the dark shadow of the adjutant. There were so many time-honoured rules and regulations that it was almost impossible to keep out of trouble; and the order 'wanted in the orderly room' became a daily occurrence and an occupational hazard. As a newly joined ensign, I was sent for by the adjutant, Captain the Hon. Thomas Vesey, who told me that now I was in the Guards I must grow a moustache.

He addressed me as he would a tiresome child, and then added the ominous warning that it was to be a 'Guards moustache and not a Charlie Chaplin'. I can still remember the hush when, a beardless seventeen, but anxious to please, I enquired: 'What colour would you like it, sir?'

Tom Vesey was a first-class soldier both in the field and on the barrack square, but, like most men small in stature, he was a martinet; he regarded ensigns as the lowest form of life, and he rarely failed to treat us accordingly. He was a magnificent soldier, but meticulous, exacting and inconsiderate.

One day he was expecting my platoon on parade. Suddenly he turned to one of my guardsmen and, pointing at me, fired: 'What's your officer's name?' The man had only recently joined the battalion, and I awaited his reply with lively interest, mixed with some trepidation, for the 'Micks' are rarely at a loss for the unexpected retort.

'Lord De Vesey,' the man replied. Tom always wore the peak of his gold-braided cap tilted well over his eyes. From where I stood, I believe I actually saw the hair on his head move upright like the bristles on a hedgehog. 'Yes, Lord De Vesey,' the man repeated.

I must explain that Ivo, Lord De Vesey, was Tom Vesey's brother, and was at that time regimental adjutant at Buckingham Gate. The two brothers were at that moment contesting in the law courts a transaction which concerned the sale of a horse that Ivo had sold to Tom. This reply, in its confused inaccuracy, was not calculated to improve my standing with Tom, who suspected I might have put the man up to it.

Often it seemed as if Tom was concentrating his sole offensive on me. Automatically I seemed to draw his fire, yet on occasion I was aware of signs of tolerance, like a weakness, a strange kind of love-hate relationship. There were other officers senior to us who were more considerate and less exacting–Tim Nugent, Gerald Hubbard, Piggie Hogg, Val Pollok and Sidney Fitz-Gerald, known as Black Fitz.

At Harrow, when my housemaster learned that I wrote verse, much was foregiven; and when Tom in his turn came to know this he seemed unconsciously to temper his professional dislike, as if he realised that, although we were moving from completely different points, together we shared the same vague yearning for the beauty and mystery of lovely intangible things.

In France I had once returned to the support lines with my company after a particularly unfortunate engagement: we had lost three officers and twenty-four other ranks. When Tom saw me alive his welcoming remark was 'Christ! It had to be you.' And yet I noticed to my surprise an almost affectionate intonation in his voice. I had still to learn that the persecutor and the persecuted are in course of time naturally drawn together in a common bond like the trainer and the lion tied to each other by the thongs of the whip.

He little realised how astonished and delighted I was myself to see him on that cold grey dawn in the support lines. I had by then conditioned myself to the prospect and acceptance of death. At that time I believed that to be an artist you not only had to live and think like one; you must also be prepared to die like one, conforming democratically to the mass pattern of death. I had not then learned that to be a poet it was not strictly necessary to write poems, but I must have already realised that death is ever-present in a poet's thoughts: for the artist death is always in the next room.

Years later, after the war, I used to meet Tom Vesey frequently at Seaford House, the London home of Margot and Tommy Howard de Walden. She was the most wonderful, original and intelligent of hostesses. By this time Tom was something in the City (he always managed to be *something* wherever he was), and the fires had cooled. Good food and the best brandy in London had mellowed him, and when I looked into his friendly blue eyes I wondered how he had ever enforced his harsh discipline on my comrades and me. They had admired, feared and hated him, but my attitude towards him must have sprung from some emotional laziness, for I realised even then that I had no talent for hating, and I have failed to acquire it since, except towards obviously loathsome things like ventriloquists or pottery figures of animals playing musical instruments and people who insist on recounting their dreams.

Tom was respected, but he never inspired the affection and loyalty felt by the whole battalion for the rather more shadowy figure of our commanding officer, the Earl of Kerry.

There was a lordly occasion, at the Commanding Officer's Orders, when Kerry had a man before him on a 'drunk' charge. Turning to the sergeant-major (for he was essentially a fair man), he asked: 'Yes, but how drunk was this man, sergeant-major?' In a lovely Wicklow brogue the answer came back: 'Drunk as a lord, my lord, and begging your pardon, my lord.'

Those of us who were young had entered the war in a light-hearted mood, and we looked on its first months as a time of high adventure. It was only later that we learned the grim reality of life in death. In our innocence and ignorance this prelude was a time of pleasure and delight, enlivened always by the wit and eccentricities of Pingo Langrishe. He had a disconcerting way of serving dinner in reverse; on the other hand, in spite of being Irish, he was the least superstitious of men, and had no hesitation in arranging a party of thirteen.

On arrival you took your place at the dining-table. When the party had all assembled, we were offered cigars, port, coffee and nuts. Dinner started with the sweet, which was followed by the entrée, then the fish and finally the soup and hors d'œuvre, the appropriate wines being served with each course. At about midnight we moved to the drawing-room for the excellent dry martinis served from a big glass jug, over which he had no more than waved the French vermouth.

After one of these dinners, I was going on with other friends to a débutante dance in Park Lane to which Pingo had not been invited. Nevertheless, since he was remarkably good-looking and deligthful company, he was always welcome wherever he appeared, so we took him with us. In the smoke-room, where he had gone to enjoy one of the long thin Havanas he habitually smoked, he discovered a man helping himself to a large whisky. Pingo followed suit, remarking that it was quite the most boring dance he had attended for a long time, whereupon the man heartily agreed, obviously delighted to meet a fellow-sufferer, and added most seriously: 'I could not have tried harder to persuade my wife not to give it.'

The Langrishes were natural Irish wits. Pingo's father once became involved in a divorce case, and the judge had occasion to ask him: 'Sir Hercules, can you honestly say that you never slept with this woman.' 'Not a wink, your honour,' was the manly reply. Many claims to this noble utterance have been laid on behalf of lesser men; but it is to Sir Hercules alone that our homage is due.

Pingo never liked Gillett, the snobbish president of the fashionable Bachelors' Club. To annoy him Pingo always mispronounced his name. One day Gillett angrily said: 'I'd like you to remember that the "G" in my name is soft, as in "gentleman".'

'Oh, I'm sorry,' Pingo replied, 'I thought it was hard, as in "bugger".'

Gillett's interest in humanity was confined to that part of it which moved in aristocratic circles. He himself had risen from humble beginnings, as they say; and the club he founded, the Bachelors' in Piccadilly, was at that time a cross between White's and Buck's. Robert Burns might, had he known him, been thinking of him when he wrote:

> No more of your titled acquaintances boast,
> Nor in what Lordly company you've been.
> An insect is but an insect at most,
> Though it crawl on the head of a Queen.

But even in war-time the Brigade of Guards was most strictly run. We wore 'plain clothes' off duty, for the Brigade never served in India so the word 'mufti' and other phrases of the barrack-room were on the Index. Morning-coat and top-hat were worn in London when the king and queen were at Buck House. We never shook hands with each other, and we used Christian names only. I mention this because in general there was more formality in those days: Christian names were used only *en famille* or between really old friends or those you had been brought up with.

We bought our clothes from the regimental tailor, and our shoes from Maxwell or Lobb. We spoke of 'London' and never 'Town', and never referred to a week-end. We were not allowed to travel on buses and were forbidden to carry parcels. We had to smoke either Turkish or Egyptian cigarettes: Péra, Orea or Balkan Sobranie, which came in china boxes. Pipes were slightly frowned upon.

It was only when the Prince of Wales insisted upon the Embassy Club stocking Gold Flake, that American tobacco was allowed to be smoked in Brigade messes; and these, when bought, had immediately to be transferred from the pack to a cigarette-case. Strangely we were allowed to wear suede shoes in uniform, and a watch-chain, preferably platinum and gold from Cartier or the Goldsmiths & Silversmiths Co. This was worn tautly stretched from one breast-pocket to the other.

In the evening we wore blue mess-kit with an inch of broad scarlet braid down the trouser-leg. Our greatcoats were steel-grey with scarlet linings. Valentine Castlerosse on one occasion arrived at Liverpool Street Station at the same time as a batch of prisoners who were wearing their German field-grey uniforms. It was fortunate for him that the cigar has always been regarded as a status-symbol by the English bourgeoisie and proles, for in his grey greatcoat Valentine was immediately mistaken for an escaped German prisoner, and, had he not been smoking a Havana about a foot long, he might easily have been torn asunder by the raging patriotic mob that swarmed about him.

One night, after dining on King's Guard at St James's Palace, Prince George Imretinsky, Jack Aird (both Grenadiers), Lord Inverclyde of the Scots Guards, Stanley Passmore, even then an eminent solicitor, and myself had taken a box at the Vaudeville. We arrived in time for the last act. We had all had an elegant sufficiency of wine, so, when George left the box and failed to return at the finale, we assumed that he had gone home. Next day we learned that he had woken up in the loo at two o'clock in the morning. Still a little uncertain as to where he was, he groped about in the pitch dark of the auditorium, feeling his way through an endless amphitheatre of seats.

At last, when he realised the situation, he had negotiated some stairs that led unrewardingly to a padlocked door to the street. At the foot of the door he noticed a letter-slot, through which, when he lay on the cement floor, he was able to view the street. Eventually a policeman strolled along but each time George tried to attract his attention, the stupid fellow looked up instead of down. At last, resigned to a situation rarely experienced by even the keenest theatregoer, he spent the rest of the night gazing at the safety curtain from a stall in the front row until released the next morning by an astonished cleaner.

George, a Cresta-champion, was the only Russian holding a commission in the British Army. Queen Alexandra was his godmother, so the Grenadiers eventually accepted him. We formed a friendship that has been precious to me throughout my life. Twice he has been my best man, and twice I have been his. When he made his wise second marriage it was to Nancy Strong, the lovely daughter of the Vicar of St Paul's, Covent Garden.

It was a rule in the Brigade, even in the first years of the war, that an officer could wear a black tie and dinner-jacket in a grill-room; but in a restaurant proper white tie and tail-coat were *de rigueur*. I was about to dine in the Savoy Grill one night when I detected a swift expression of invitation in the eyes of a girl passing through the foyer to the restaurant. She was so beautiful that I decided immediately that I must meet her; but, alas, I was wearing a dinner-jacket. By a fortunate chance Jackie Aird happened to be dining in the restaurant. Buttonholing him in the foyer, I persuaded him to exchange his tail-coat for my dinner-jacket to enable me to enter the restaurant, where I could at least apprise the girl of my continued existence.

Jackie had, and still has, a tall graceful figure, while mine was, and still is, the exact opposite. He was agreeable to my suggestion if I promised not to be too long, as he had not yet dined. I explained that I just wanted to meet the girl and, if lucky, to have one dance with her.

When, eventually, I presented myself as a complete stranger at her table she made no attempt to suppress her laughter, in which all the party joined: on the short journey from the men's room to the restaurant Jackie's tail-coat had burst at the seams, the diamond and onyx buttons in his white waistcoat, under extreme tension, no longer functioned, and his coat-tails hung to my ankles. But this *belle dame avec merci* had a place made for me, and a glass of champagne was put in my hand. I was immediately accepted as one of the party.

In the meantime Jackie had gone into the American Bar. Here apparently, his appearance in my dinner-jacket excited so much curiosity and amusement that he had been forced to retreat to the men's room, there to await my return. Here, an hour later, I discovered him in a state of near-starvation. It was charmingly typical of him that I was greeted only with the gentle rebuke: 'That was the hell of a long dance.'

Neither Jackie nor I realised that the long dance I had enjoyed with the dreamy girl was to be the last of its sort. From now on it was to be the *danse macabre* for us and a thousand others.

A few days later I was posted to the 2nd Battalion, in command
C2

of a platoon. On the death of old Lord Roberts of Kandahar, Field-Marshal Lord Kitchener of Khartoum, who began his military career as a sapper, was appointed Colonel of the Irish Guards, and in this capacity he inspected the battalion on 13 August 1915. After introductions, and drinking port in the mess, we were grouped outside with him for the customary photograph.

As one of the junior ensigns, I was standing next to John Kipling, the son of Rudyard Kipling, on a form in the back row. As usual, John was superbly smart, for he was meticulous about his appearance. Kitchener was seated between Lord Kerry and our commanding officer, the Hon. L. J. P. Butler. Unfortunately John, from his superior height, had noticed a grease-spot on the Field-Marshal's cap, which he immediately pointed to; and in the intense hush which precedes the taking of a photograph, his resonant voice broke the silence: 'I told you, Rupert, that Kitchener would never made a guardsman.'

After the photograph had been taken we made a quick get-away; we suspected an immediate summons to the Orderly Room. Unwittingly, by speaking my name, John had involved me, too; but fortunately the Kiplings' Rolls was waiting to take us down to Bateman's.

When I had first joined the regiment John had introduced me to his parents and his delightful schoolgirl sister, Elsie. The battalion was now under embarkation orders, so this was the last opportunity any of us had to go home. I was to go down to Bateman's with John, and the old Rolls, always known as 'the ensigns' car', would drive me back to London to take leave of own my parents and family.

Father seriously believed that it was possible to catch typhoid fever from walking over a drain. I remember him once turning to me in a ferociously smelly alley in Cairo and demanding a cigarette. I found him one with trepidation. I was only ten at the time, and apparently he knew that I had already begun smoking on the sly. I think I must have inherited this highly sensitive sense of smell, because smells spark off my memories; thus the odour, so deeply satisfying, of old furniture that has stood for a

lifetime on parquet floors and of ash logs burning in a giant
fireplace will always take my mind back to Bateman's, the
Kipling home.

That summer evening the old house stood so peacefully in its
Sussex valley it was as though the news of a war in Europe had
never reached it. I stayed for an hour, then made my farewells to
these dear people who had been so kind to me. I too was going
home to say even more poignant farewells; but it never occurred
to me that for John this was the last night he would ever spend
in the old house with those he loved so well.

On 16 August 1915 the battalion entrained at Brentwood
Station for Waterloo *en route* for embarkation at Southampton.
Mother was at Warley Barracks to see me off, fussing about my
socks and handkerchiefs, loving and a little cross, just as she had
always been when, the holidays over, she had shepherded me
with the others to the train that would take us back to school.

Father was at Waterloo. It was out of drinking-hours (recently
introduced) and he was very annoyed when the woman in
the buffet refused to serve us. He was completely unaccustomed
to people saying 'no' to him. He had a dominating personality,
but he was a dangerous man to fool with, because he was strong
with men, even if he was too susceptible to women; but when he
wished he could be remarkably persuasive; so, without too
much effort, we had our farewell drink together. The only other
thing I remember is that he called to me as the train moved out:
'I've arranged for a case of whisky to be sent to the mess every
fortnight.'

As we steamed out of the station he stood, tall and erect in his
uniform, head and shoulders above the crowd, surely a prince
among men.

5

The Trumpet Calls . . . There is
Throats to be Cut

WHEN I embarked in the *Viper* for Le Havre I was just
eighteen years of age and the proud holder of a
commission in His Majesty's Fourth Regiment of Foot
Guards, *corps d'élite* of the British Army.

Our prime loyalty as soldiers was to the person of the monarch,
King George V; and it was against his enemies rather than in
response to patriotic impulse – we were an Irish regiment
anyway – that we sailed for that *terra incognita*, 'the Front'.

For almost a year at Warley I had 'prepared for war'; but it
was for a war fought in story-books rather than the realities of
the high explosives, poison gas and barbed wire that were
awaiting us. Equipping myself for the story-book conflict had
been a pleasant and exciting business. Among other essentials,
I had acquired a folding canvas bed with blankets, a canvas
wash-basin on a wooden tripod, a canvas bath and bucket and a
canvas folding chair. The canvas was of the stoutest, and the
timber of the weightiest and most durable; effective transporta-
tion to the scene of conflict would have needed a mule-train.

Added to these were the more personal items suggested to me
as necessary for the destruction of the 'Hun', most of them
expensive and so obtainable at Asprey's or Finnigan's in Bond
Street. At these excellent establishments I acquired the following:
a pair of field-glasses to bring the enemy under close observation
before joining battle; a highly intricate compass, together with
maps of Belgium and northern France, all contained in luxuriously

smelling leather with my initials stamped thereon; a felt-enwrapped water-bottle sustained by a shoulder-strap and so shaped that it would not unduly bruise the buttocks when on the march. My revolver and holster were, I believe, supplied by the Ordnance Corps, but my Sam Browne belt, so lovingly polished by my servant, I bought myself. This ingenious piece of equipment, apart from what was hung or attached to it on my back and shoulders also took the weight of the frog that secured my sword.

The sword I obtained, of course, from Wilkinson of Pall Mall. While there engaged in its selection I happened to see a smaller lighter version of the massive weapon the salesman was urging upon me; and I expressed my preference for it.

'Oh no, sir!' he cried, deeply shocked. '*This* is the regulation sword. That is a *dress* sword – a court sword.'

However, I insisted on the court sword and ordered one to be forged and the date and my initials engraved on the blade. This shocking breach of the regulations escaped even the blue sea-bird eye of Tom Vesey, who must sometimes have lain awake wondering why I, of all the ensigns the most unlikely, displayed the greatest dexterity in sheathing and unsheathing the flashing blade. After the war I gave it to my brother Tristram, who later became Colonel in the Irish Guards: it is now owned by his son, Patrick, of the regiment, and still, I hope, goes unnoticed in comparative peace as in total war.

Johns & Pegg made my khaki uniform. The jacket, its small bronze buttons stitched in groups of four, and with an ensign's single star on the epaulettes, was cut with the pockets unpleated to ensure close fit to the lower garment, a species of baggy knickerbockers tailored to a precise regulation length and moulded to the calves by a smooth spiralling of Fox's patent puttees.

Cater's supplied me with caps: they had black leather peaks edged with braided gold and bore the cross of St Patrick encircled by a silver ribbon with the motto: 'Quis Separabit?'

I used the field-glasses once only before they were blasted off me. I can only hope that they were later found and proved their worth at some subsequent Derby, Ascot Gold Cup or Cambridgeshire. Before they were parted from me, however, I was

'vouchsafed' one glimpse of the wire bristling round the Hohenzollern redoubt at Loos, draped with the bodies of the gallant
Highland Division, their kilts caught high in the barbs, and
buttocks black and a-buzz with flies. The compass I lost at a
card-game a few days after landing in France. The revolver I
somehow retained, but never fired: it had a trigger that would
have taxed the combined strengths of Alexander and Hercules,
not to mention Hector and Lysander and such great men as
these, let alone a stripling of eighteen.

What happened to the map-case, I have no idea. In any event
it would have been useless, as was most of this equipment
dreamed up, I suppose, by some dear old boy in the War Office.
Going to the wars in 1914–18 was a costly business, but to us,
the nurslings of 'Pax Britannica', war was to be the test of
manhood.

We had no strong feelings about what the politicians called
'the rape of little Belgium'. We were afraid of one thing only –
that we would not be there to 'see the fun', believing that any
day it might be over. The youth of Germany had much the same
attitude: the German Crown Prince, 'Little Willie', drank to
'Ein frischer, fröhlicher Krieg' – a brisk and merry war.

I myself had nothing against the Germans, apart from their
alleged addiction to raping nuns, which was anyway the
traditional habit of brutal continental soldiery on the march.
With their love of brass bands and drumbeats, it was not
surprising that they were a warlike people, especially with an
emperor at their head who wore his helmet eagle-crowned. I had
been told that 'Kaiser Bill' had come over for Queen Victoria's
funeral, a gallant sorrowing grandson with the tears streaming
down his face, and that it was in his arms that she had died. His
moustache was too long and too upturned, and obviously he was
no more than every other inch a gentleman, but surely the decent
(English) side of his character would eventually prevail. Alas, it
did not. In my lifetime 'Kaiser Bill' with his fierce moustache
and, twenty years later, Hitler with his little one were both to
become representatives of that strangest Germanic mixture, the
ridiculous and the sinister.

Already in London the wounded were to be seen in the streets. They were a race who had been to – and miraculously returned from – another world, a vague area mysteriously known as 'the Front'. It was to us, the newly recruited, a romantic Valhalla lying beyond the shores of France, peopled with heroes in immaculate uniforms who charged the enemy with flashing swords and who, occasionally, 'fell' to the accompaniment of the 'music of the guns'.

But the truth of all this, as from the *Viper*'s decks we watched the Channel waters swishing by, we knew nothing except that we were sure 'to see the fun' before it was over and that on the approaching shores there would be wine awaiting us and romantic encounters with lovely French girls.

This last possibility ranked high among our expectations. The England of 1915 was not the sexually permissive society it has since so surprisingly become. To sleep with a girl of one's own age and class was then not only practically impossible, but quite unthinkable. It 'ruined them for marriage'; so the needs of a licentious soldiery had to be catered for elsewhere, with discretion, or, if you will, a decent hypocrisy.

The Brigade used to enjoy the hospitality of a charming Irishwoman known as 'Mrs Fitz', who ran a house, or rather establishment, in Clarges Street. It was furnished, as was her person, in an opulent Edwardian style and conducted with great etiquette and strict regard to rank and privilege.

A field-officer would be shown by a hatchet-faced parlourmaid to the drawing-room; a mere lieutenant or lowly ensign to a room on the ground floor; but wherever it happened to be it would have a well-stuffed sofa and gilt chairs with antimacassars facing a fireplace above which hung a 'Stag at Bay' or 'Charge of the Light Brigade'. Here one would be introduced to young ladies whose attitude to life and love differed vastly from those one met at the deb-dances, which were still taking place, but in a rather tense 'Eve of Waterloo' atmosphere. 'Mrs Fitz', whom death has fortunately spared from witnessing the present unprofessional looseness of manners and morals, kept open house from 6 p.m. to 3 a.m., except on Sundays, certain feast-days, royal nuptials and bereavements, and the Fourth of June, when she visited her son at Eton.

If I have hitherto given the impression that life as an ensign in the Guards was one of frivolity and pleasure, this is only because it is that brief part of it I like to remember. The rest and ninety-nine per cent of it was hell. To hold a commission in the Guards carried no privileges – quite the contrary. We were bullied, bawled at, hounded and humiliated by the sergeant-major, drill sergeants and officers – in front of our men – in a way that would never have been tolerated by the quick-tempered Irish in the ranks; but it was an ancient rite, handed down from generation to generation, that somehow turned us into guardsmen. Our soldiers, I knew, felt profoundly sorry for us; but, oddly, they admired the way we stuck it, as men would doing great penances for unnamed mysterious sins; and they tried to temper our misery with their loyal warmth. To compensate, we were all magnificently fit.

The inadequacies of our approach and training to mass and static warfare were common to all British regiments, which had never formed an army in the continental sense, but rather a force to police an empire and, in our own special case, to guard the person of the monarch against his enemies.

If ignorance of the true nature of the war was widespread in the forces, among the civilians it was total. True, in those early days, wounded had begun to appear in the streets, but they were seen not as men who had been subjected to gross indignities in a war that really didn't make sense, but as romantic heroes.

Even death had its palliative: 'killed in action' had a nobler, more satisfying ring about it than the banal obituaries of peace: 'passed away' (from kidney disease or pox); 'taken from us' (by senility). When the death 'in action' of my uncle Ambrose was announced I know that Father was secretly proud he should have died that way.

It was with these illusions, thus equipped, and in high spirits that I and my comrades disembarked at Le Havre; and then entrained (*hommes 40, chevaux 8*) for 'the line'. At Lumbres, the railhead, we detrained and set out to march to battle along the never-ending French *pavé*. The only transport then considered fit for infantry was one pair of hob-nailed ammunition boots per man. Only field-officers were mounted, and the transport was mule-drawn. We sang as we marched, soldiers' bawdy songs, mile after mile, day after day.

At the end of each day's march I could have dropped exhausted wherever the halt was made and slept for ever; but I had to see to it that my men were fed, inspect their feet – it was our pride that no man should fall out – and install them in whatever shelter was available. They were even wearier and more footsore than I: they squatted on their packs with drooping heads like winded horses.

Then suddenly the news would quickly pass through all the battalion like a breath of Ireland that Alex was to dance. This was Harold Alexander, the future field-marshal, later Earl Alexander of Tunis, elder brother of my schoolfriend. When the moment came the entire battalion would be seated round the platform, some with bottles of unaccustomed vino, but all quietly as became men who had marched their twenty-five miles. Each knew that a man they loved, their commander who had marched with them footsore step for step, was ready to dance for their delight.

His performance had an electrifying effect on them. Alex was always the complete individualist and so he wore a hat with the upper part elevated and pressed back *à la Russe* and beneath it his fair moustache and his Tsar-like appearance when he mounted the platform held his footsore audience spellbound. It was as if we were about to see a Polovtsian dance to the music of Borodin, to the resin perfume of pine-trees – it was only with the discordant wail of the squeeze box and the cries of the men that one realised that the dance was the nostalgic jig and the music was the music of the defiant Gael.

There Alex would be 'steppin' ', on an improvised wooden platform, head erect, arms and body rigid, and feet tapping and lifting and leaping and crossing and clicking like objects with a life of their own, as the lads in rural Ireland jig at the cross-roads after Mass on Sundays. And the men would stand enthralled, their weariness cast off, stamping their feet and clapping their hands and uttering wild Gaelic yells and battles-cries to the tap of their feet.

Alex was a man of indescribable charm and courage, highly strung and sensitive and of luminous intelligence. His men, as they say, worshipped him, although he kept the strictest discipline, and this not blindly, but in a kind of highly moral way.

Alex knew everything; he had been in it from the beginning. He was steeped in the squalor of war and yet, unlike most men he rose above it. He was a disciplinarian in the true sense of judging between right and wrong. Often he would go out on night patrol with his orderly. He did this partly, I believe, to keep his nerve and then maybe because he could gain information. To be Alex's orderly a man had to be adventurous, courageous and tough.

On one occasion he captured a German and as he intended crawling closer to the enemy trenches he ordered the man to stay behind him to guard the prisoner, who was badly needed for interrogation. A few minutes later he was surprised by his orderly crawling up beside him, whispering that the prisoner had begun to make trouble, so he had silently garrotted him.

'I finished him off, sir, with my pull-through,' he said.

On their return Alex at once put the strangler, a trusted friend, on a disobedience charge. This was at a time when, God knows, life was cheap and discipline inclined to be stretched to meet the occasion. There could, however, be no tampering with discipline in the Brigade of Guards. We responded to the word of command as a reflex action.

Once the C.O. of a Guards battalion rode his mount before a parade of officers and men, about to give the order 'Present Arms'. He screamed out 'Bat-talion, Pre-sent...' and all stood, as they say, waiting for the executive word of command: 'Arms'; when suddenly his horse whinnied 'Whee-ee-ee'; and as one man, in perfect unison, hands smacked against rifle-stocks, swords and bayonets flashed, and the battalion came to the 'Present'.

There were other men touched with genius in our ranks: the

Sitwells in the Grenadiers and Stephen Graham in the Scots Guards. In the Irish Guards were Valentine Williams (the Ian Fleming of his era), Count John de Salis, H. Marion-Crawford, Valentine Castlerosse. I little knew at the time that the blue-eyed Guardsman No. 68732, registered in the regiment under an assumed name as Trained Soldier Ganley, was Liam O'Flaherty, with whom I was later to form a lasting friendship. Apart from his novels *The Informer* and *The Puritan* and his autobiography, *Shame the Devil*, this great Irish writer's animal stories have surely never been surpassed, even by W. H. Hudson. After being gassed and wounded, Liam went back to Ireland to exercise his martial skill against the British in the cause of Irish freedom.

We marched on; it was during the spell from Acquin to Dohem that Tom Vesey noticed an oblong-shaped canvas bag in the transport wagon. Nothing escaped him. He ordered the canvas bag to be ripped off, to disclose in all its nakedness my pigskin suitcase. It contained shirts, a dressing-gown, under-clothes, bedroom slippers, ivory brushes, a bottle of Hill's C.A.R. hair-oil, two boxes of Roger et Gallet's soap, *David Copperfield* and a copy of Voltaire's *Candide*. In short, those things which represented my last contact with another world, symbols of a civilised life.

The case was flung to the side of the road, and I never saw it again, 'You haven't the makings of a soldier, Rupert,' Tom said to me, sadly.

'Perhaps not, but I'll make a better civilian than you,' I muttered to myself, because it was not always wise to speak too clearly to Tom.

By this time we all knew that we were going straight into the Battle of Loos. On 27 September the regimental diaries record that the battalion 'had now been on foot or livelily awake for forty-eight hours . . . It remained for them merely to go into the fight . . .'

This for most of us was our 'baptism of fire'. At first it was shrapnel kicking up earth and sparking the *pavé*; but as we moved forward to Chalk-Pit Wood, heavy shells started landing with alarming precision and regularity. I believe I would have been even more afraid than I was had the noise and the increasing roar not seemed to deafen my fears.

Suddenly a blinding flash lit up my entire world, stars exploded in my eyes and a mighty wind, charged with the acrid stench of high explosive, channelled me through a vaulted echoing cavern. I was riding the night, driving into a mirage of the past, present and future, then flung into total darkness.

Kipling, in his *The Irish Guards in the Great War*, wrote: 'Captain and the Adjutant the Hon. T. E. Vesey . . . and 2nd Lieutenants Sassoon and Grayson were wounded, the last being blown up by a shell.'

So Tom was returned to England with me; for all I know he was in the same hospital at Le Tréport and on the same ship to Southampton. Some strange rhythm seemed to govern our lives so that though we were always marching together we were rarely in step.

In France the regiment were still burying their dead when through the grapevine I heard the news that froze my heart: John Kipling had been reported missing.

6

The Master of Bateman's

As I lay in my hospital bed and closed my eyes I could at will seem to see Rudyard Kipling, a short, wiry, alert man with steely blue eyes peering through his spectacles under bushy eyebrows and bald head, firm chin poked forward. His glasses were part of him, as headlights are part of a car. At school he was known as 'gigs', after the lamps on each side of a gig. He was pedantically neat, with a butterfly-collar and dark tie, pinned neatly beneath his high-buttoned waistcoat.

Mrs Kipling chose his clothes, his ties, shirts and shoes as she chose his publishers, agents and bankers; and those who didn't know whispered that she chose his friends as carefully. She was everything to him; the mother of his children, wife, secretary, nurse, banker and literary adviser, from the time they were married at All Souls', Langham Place (the pepperpot, he called it), until his death.

Even at the time I realised that I was being more fortunate than I deserved in being honoured with his friendship. Any charm of manner I might have had could hardly made up for my instability, which must have been very apparent.

He gave his greatest attention to young people. The friends who came to Bateman's were rarely middle-aged. He liked the old if they were interesting, but the young he liked because they were young.

Once when I was staying at Bateman's I had a sudden longing to see a little dancer I knew, so I sent a telegram to tell her I would be in London. I made the unnecessary excuse to the Kiplings that I had an appointment with my dentist. On my return the following day, Rudyard Kipling handed me an open telegram. His eyebrows were raised and his eyes were twinkling. 'I hope the dentist didn't hurt too much, old man,' he said. The telegram he handed me read: 'Meet me at stage door 5.30 love Irene.'

In London the Kiplings kept open suite in their old-fashioned rooms at Brown's, in Dover Street. Since his first visit to London he never stayed at any other hotel; he had grown old with it, with the servants and with the wine in its cellars. The head-waiter, Mr Holmes, who had the manners and dignity of a bishop, was one of our favourites; and there was a Mr Nice, the hall-porter, about whom Kipling used to say: 'If Nice was put in charge of the Foreign Office there would never be another European war.'

On week-end leave from barracks, John and I usually motored down to Bateman's. This was the corner of England that during his years in India Kipling must have dreamed of; this was the soil of England, an Englishman's heritage. It is a mellow sandstone house, gabled, with mullioned windows and high sixteenth-century brick chimneys. Close by there is the farm and an oast-house with a warm russet-coloured roof.

It has a formal English garden with a stone-flagged lily pond, and beyond that lay his pastureland. He walked his land and felt it under his feet. He trod the grassy paths or pottered about by the flood-water in the meadow. At Bateman's he had all the things that he had longed for, even to an English river wandering through his land.

Seated at the long refectory table in his study he could hear the plovers cry and watch the pigeons flapping home to the woods that lined the valley, and he could enjoy the glorious music of his own farm-horses splashing down the lane.

I wonder whether the realisation of his dream had eluded him. It seemed to me that in spite of his intense interest in everything to do with country life he was essentially a man of the cities. In the village he was never popular. The locals were prepared to respect the no-man's-land with which he liked to surround himself, so they left him alone, possibly too much alone. Kipling was never more than a man who lived in Sussex, though I think in his heart he longed to have been a Sussex man.

It was as if he knew that he was always to be a wanderer. His name on his farm-carts might well have been a gesture of definance: 'R. Kipling, Bateman's, Burwash'. He wished at times to be the farmer, when all the time he was never anything but the writer.

When you were with him you had to be lightning quick with your answers, for he was never slow in supplying one himself. An American woman was once complimenting him on his wide vocabulary. 'Mr Kipling,' she said, 'has it ever occurred to you that the only word in the English language where s-u is pronounced as s-h-u is the word sugar?'

'Sure,' he said, smiling.

'The man we've been speaking to', he told me one day, 'is the last of five generations of hedgers.' He then proceeded to give a brilliant exposition of hedging and ditching.

It was on one of his walks along the narrow Sussex lanes that a farm-cart turning abruptly into a field gave him the idea of a story of detection. He wrote it immediately on returning to Bateman's, but, not satisfied with it, put it aside. 'Never destroy anything you write,' he advised me, for he knew that it was my intention when the war was over to be a writer. 'Put it into cold storage; you'll use it one day in some form.'

R.K. loved bonfires. Together we devised a successful technique for lighting them. Once he telegraphed me: 'Your presence required at Bateman's have bonfire stop no bon.' He could never manage to keep blazing those he lit himself.

It was not long before Lady Edward Cecil, a great friend of the Kiplings, came to visit me in the hospital. She wanted to know about John, everything I could tell her. That was little because there was little to tell, and I was still suffering from the effects of concussion. But this was about the time I myself first had heard about John being missing. I was filled with a great sadness. I had lost a close friend and the regiment a grand officer.

I was able to tell her only of how we awaited the grey dawn and of the casually tense trivialities before we went into action. It was little comfort to grieving parents. The next day Kipling came to see me himself: it was solely out of friendship and loyalty to John. He already knew I had nothing to tell him.

He was holding himself under control, but the light had gone from his eyes. I was able to make a suggestion that might give the family hope, or help them over the period of first shock. The Prince of Wales was attached to the Staff of Lord Cavan, who commanded the Guards Division. He had a roving commission of which he took full advantage, moving among the troops from one end of our lines to the other. He was a familiar and much-loved figure. I suggested to Kipling that he was the one man who had the opportunity and authority to investigate the disappearance of one particular man in a battle where the dead and wounded were being counted in their thousands. The question was: would he do it? Nothing could be lost by asking him. But the answer was really never in doubt: the prince was a great-hearted man. A few days later I received this letter by hand-of-officer:

H.Q. Guards Div.
October 15, 1916

Dear Grayson,

Many thanks for your letter. I must apologise for the long delay of this answer, but it hasn't been easy to get hold of any information regarding Kipling.

My answer is the enclosed note from Bird, who, I understand, was his company commander: I wrote to him as I thought he would know as much as anyone, and then I saw Father Knapp yesterday, whose story was much the same as Bird's in every detail. We can but trust he is a prisoner.

Your 1st Battalion had most unfortunate casualties last week, losing the C.O. and the adjutant wounded, poor Gore-Langton and Father Gwynne, the R.C. chaplain, killed. It was a shell in the H.Q. dug-out; the very worst luck.

I hope you are getting on well and will soon be out of hospital.

I am sorry I can't tell you more about Kipling, but I have done my best.

Yours very sincerely,
EDWARD

Valentine Castlerosse, unaware that John had that day been reported missing, happened to call in at Bateman's. The day passed pleasantly, for Valentine was a wit and a brilliant conversationalist, and Kipling was showing his usual grip of affairs and arriving at conclusions with his crystal-clear reasoning. Then the time came for Valentine to leave.

'I'm off to France, so I'll be seeing John, and I'll tell him that I've seen you.' Kipling paused in his walk, looked Valentine straight in the face, and in a great voice that rang out like a trumpet, cried: '*He is missing.*'

About this time he wrote to me:

Bateman's, Burwash, Sussex.

I am sorry to learn – though it isn't in the least surprising seeing what you have gone through, that you are still a bit shaken up. However, I can assure you for your consolation that with your youth and temperament you will come through without damage. It is often the very strength of a young man kicking against the accident or shock to his body that makes him feel so infernally wretched. Older men don't, as they imagine, feel shock so much, that only means that they haven't the elasticity.

So when you are feeling like 'three penn'orth of tripe' as John used to say, remember that it isn't your weakness declaring itself but your strength coming back. I was never hoisted by a shell but I've been rather ill once in my life when I was young, and I know.

The serious matter seems to me the loss of your dog. A man has a feeling about a dog which is quite apart from other feelings. I only wish I had one that I could venture to recommend to fill the old one's place: but our animal Jack is rather a mongrel hound of reserved character and absolutely no morals. He began life as a poacher, under the able tuition of his sister, a brown and white rough-haired terrier bitch. And if ever that expressive word exactly expressed a lady, it did in her case. I have fished Jack out of rabbit wires in the woods at eleven o'clock at night and seen him sneak off for fresh trouble next morning. Obviously *he's* no good.

My own idea would be a sealyham. There isn't a wiser or more gentlemanly breed alive, and they are good for most things up to badgers.

Your mother says that when you feel fitter you will come down here, and that prospect is making us happy.

There is a literary career open for you when you feel like it. I do a bit at it myself. It is the manufacture of scrap-books for the wounded in hospital. Observe the process. You take a mass of magazines, weekly papers, *John Bulls, Life, Punch,* etc., – anything with fairly vulgar pictures and fairly vulgar jokes. You cut out the pictures, from ads of motor bikes to beautiful females without clothes (the hospitals like this) and you mix in the vulgar jokes in the proportion of about 3 to 5. Then you take 12 sheets, not more, of brown paper and gum the resulting mixture on to 'em. Sometimes one makes a refined scrapbook – pretty girls and squashy verses – for a delicate soul. Otherwise one goes in for purely comic effects. The curious thing is that a man who isn't equal to reading gets a sort of languid pleasure from turning over the collection. The pictures remind him of civil life and most men are keen on ads of cars, motor boats, etc.

Elsie invented this idea but they are called R.K. scrap-books. There is a great deal more art in making them than you would imagine. You'll probably have to make or help make some at Bateman's.

If this disgusts you let me know.

I've been among some of our ships lately – down in a submarine and so on and am now trying to write out any impressions. It was a most interesting time.

With all our best and warmest greetings to you,

believe me,

Yours sincerely,

RUDYARD KIPLING

Remember what I told you, the next time you feel more than usually wretched. 'There are many liars but there are no liars like our own sensations.' I forget where that comes from but it is true.

Sorrow had eaten deep into Kipling's heart. He was quieter and seemed to lean more and more on his beloved Carrie. He kept alive for a long time the hope that John might still be living, but it was not to be. Losing him was a crushing blow from which he never entirely recovered.

Carrie was never far from his side and undoubtedly influenced him in everything he did. He rarely told a story that he did not call on her to finish. Added to her courage, she had an acute sense of humour, and together at table they passed the conversation from one to the other like a ball in a juggler's act. She invariably interspersed her talk, which never failed to be lively, with a neat little cough followed by a most infectious laugh.

I remember one winter evening we were compiling R.K. scrapbooks, sitting in front of the great log-fire in the hall – the ashes used to be kept for about a month and formed a bed on which lay the sweet-smelling timber. Suddenly, I saw something glitter. With a pair of tongs I fished out a diamond bracelet. Mrs Kipling was both delighted and embarrassed, because she had already claimed on the insurance for its loss.

At this time Kipling seldom went to London. He spent long hours at his work-table. In 'A Nativity' he expressed his overwhelming loss and the barren content of his life. Two verses read:

> *The Cross was raised on high;*
> *The Mother grieved beside –*
> 'But the Mother saw Him die
> And took Him when he died. . . .'

> 'Is it well with the child, is it well?'
> The waiting mother prayed.
> 'For I knew not how he fell
> And I know not where he is laid'. . . .

But despite the bitter memory of John, 'missing', Kipling intimated – to our delight – at the end of November 1916 that he and Carrie would be at the christening ceremony of Ronald, Denys's brand-new son and heir. It was typical of him that he should carry out his duties as one of the godfathers at such a time. The other godfather was Robert Hichens, author of *The Garden of Allah, Bella Donna* and many other first-class stories.

Kipling had a highly developed sense of the ludicrous, and at many of the rather pompous ceremonies at which he had to appear he must have found it difficult to suppress his mirth, but this particular occasion presented – fortunately or unfortunately – an outlet for a mischievous angle of his humour which made him so beloved of young people. And it happened, as the storytellers say, in this wise.

Turner had gone into hospital with a minor ailment, so it became necessary to engage a temporary butler. At that time menservants were at a premium, and people had to accept whoever was sent by the all-powerful Mrs Hunt, who ran an agency for domestic servants in Brompton Road. Those available had been rejected by the two services for various reasons, and were deemed useless even as cannon-fodder. Hence the arrival one day of Mr Ogle, who was to act (on his flat feet) as Turner's stand-in.

The first thing that impressed one about Ogle was that he looked the part. He was possibly a little too tall and good-looking in a rather foolish way, but was obviously the perfect butler. He made no hurried or jerky movements, and everything he did was perfectly timed. When he walked, flat-footed or not, he swayed gently from side to side with the lingering grace of a retired *maître de ballet*. If his voice was at times embarrassingly loud, with every syllable over-emphasised, it was because he appeared to be under the impression that he was addressing a vast assembly. He used rather grand expressions to which we were not accustomed, such as 'The carriage awaits without, madam', 'Will you partake of a sherry wine, sir?', 'Your theatre tickets are held in the vestibule, or what you would call the rotunda, sir', and once when opening a window he said, 'I hope I am not admitting of the draught, sir.' It was impossible not to like him, although the really remarkable feature about him was that the unhurried dignity with which he moved was within what must have been a self-generated aura of concentrated alcohol.

Father, who was Director of Ship Repairs (Foreign), was in Rome, and Mother was running a soldiers' convalescent home in Anglesey, so Denys – in uniform – and his grey-eyed wife, Elsie, were host and hostess at the party. We knew that Kipling would want to meet people out of the regiment who had known John, so Denys arranged to bring along anyone from Warley who was available, and I was to invite a few young writers.

For some reason the christening ceremony took longer than was anticipated, so that when we arrived home the party was already in full swing. I noticed immediately that Brian and Tristram, who were up from Harrow, were not looking very happy. Champagne was being served in the large dining-room. I could see from the corner of my eye that there were a number of ensigns and subalterns there with several of my exquisite sisters and their girl-friends. Also there was Dick Rawlinson, my future brother-in-law, who years later was to collaborate with Kipling in adapting his books for radio and the screen. Suddenly I realised that pandemonium was detonating from the direction of the tapestry screen at the end of the room behind which Ogle was officiating. No one seemed unduly worried, but it was impossible to ignore the crash-bang-crackle-crunch of shattering glass. This had increased since our arrival, so that our guests were shouting at each other in order to be heard. Robert Hichens was trying to talk to Mrs Kipling and John Knittel. John de Salis and Valentine Williams, favourites of Kipling's, were trying to make themselves heard above the clamour. Pingo Langrishe, now seconded from the regiment, Pat Ogilvy and Kenneth Schweder, deafened into retreat, were moving into a distant corner. Fortunately the flow of champagne was constant, so my writing friends seemed quite contented to appraise each other through half-closed eyes, a form of behaviour that was to become a notable feature of all literary parties. But Kipling had different ideas, and I saw him signalling me to join him. He had positioned himself so he could see what was going on behind the screen, Gleefully he hissed, 'This is something you mustn't miss.'

For no accountable reason Ogle was awkwardly squeezing Jimmy, the fourteen-year-old 'Buttons' into the service lift, which then descended. Needless to say it was intended for plates, glasses and cutlery and glasses only. A moment later, after much pulling on the guide rope, the lift reappeared with Jimmy hugging an armful of bottles, which Ogle immediately seized. Next he proceeded to knock off the head of each bottle in turn on a marble-topped sideboard. This done, he fountained, none too accurately, a bubbling cascade of champagne over a silver tray closely packed with glasses. There was no sense of individual attention. Each glass took its chance with the next, the only respite being when Ogle stopped to re-entrench his flat feet more firmly and noisily in the litter of broken glass and crushed ice. But he was soon back on the job of pouring and swaying, bottle-breaking, cascading, pouring and swaying.

There was no point in interfering in his merciless treatment of the bottles as the supply of champagne kept circulating, however unorthodox the method. In my troubled mind the whole performance was only disturbing because it was so completely out of character with the little one knew of Ogle. Had I suddenly seen the Venus de Milo with arms and the tower of Pisa vertical, I couldn't have been more astonished.

I had never seen Kipling more delighted. He was enjoying it like a schoolboy at a circus. 'There's a story here somewhere, old man,' he whispered eagerly.

Now Ogle's voice had risen above the cachinnation and hub-bub as he screamed his instructions to the champagne-drenched Jimmy, who was still holding the tray. Now I noticed with alarm that he was shouting in a broad cockney accent. What fresh surprise had he in store? He was pointing a lively finger at the glasses. 'That's for the kid's ma . . . That's for its father, which art in uniform . . . Those two are for the writer blokes . . . and the rest for the brutal soldiery. 'Urry, as we'll need another dozen up toot sweet and the tooter the sweeter, Jimmy.'

'Ye gods,' Kipling whispered. 'What a quartermaster-general he'd have made!'

When I went down to Bateman's a few days later I explained that we had learned that Ogle was actually an actor condemned to play nothing but butler parts, when his heart yearned to play Hamlet. But it might be said that it was Ogle who brought down the house on that famous afternoon, for after the party had broken up – unbeknown to him – in a moment of supreme confidence he had lifted a tray full of loaded glasses on the flat of his hand, shoulder high, and advanced, no doubt swaying slightly, centre stage, to take his call. It might have been the shock of seeing the house empty and the audience fled or simply a ridge in the carpet, but he had fallen, and like all great men from a great height. Some time later we found him among the debris, sleeping as peacefully as the sweet prince of his dreams.

Often I used to sit with Kipling in his workroom while he wrote. I never saw a page of manuscript that he had not decorated with little pictures down the wide margin. These little doodle-sketches were the work of an artist: 'Something my fore-bears bequeathed to me,' he said one day, for his father, Lock-wood Kipling, was a fine draughtsman.

Over the years I learned a great deal about many things in that mellow book-lined room with its strong smell of old books and bees-wax. He would talk on every kind of subject

in his unique way, a spicy mixture of biblical invocation and
barrack-room slang. He would take a volume from the shelves
and read passages that appealed to him, but his favourite
reading was The Book, and his knowledge of it was tremen-
dous.

Kipling would often play with his beloved Aberdeens, but
only occasionally would he take a complete day off: then he
would say: 'When I know nothing, old man, I do nothing.'
His voice was always soft, but when he wished to impress you
it would drop to a stage-whisper.

It was my task to burn the contents of the waste-paper
basket. He had an intense dislike of his fame being exploited
and took every precaution that none of his manuscripts should
fall into the hands of people who would sell them to collectors,
nor did he write to anyone who would be likely to sell his letters.

I was at Bateman's when he wrote 'The Vineyard', the poem
that gave so much offence to the Americans:

> At the eleventh hour he came,
> But his wages were the same
> As ours who all day long had trod
> The wine-press of the wrath of God.

He certainly showed little affection for America, though at
one time he might have made his home in Vermont, New England.
After a world tour he decided to settle there; he built himself a
house and it was in Vermont that he meant to live. A quarrel
followed with his charming, happy-go-lucky brother-in-law
Beatty Balestier. Kipling went to law. Though he won the case,
which, I believe, was one of slander and assault, this incident
soured him for American life.

The Kiplings never fitted into the parochial way of life in
Vermont. Carrie had already become anglicised, and small-
town life would never have suited her for long. It was while he
was in Vermont that he heard of the death of his great friend
and second brother-in-law, Wolcott Balestier, with whom
he collaborated in writing *The Naulahka*. It is not difficult to

understand how this sequence of events should have turned him against America and the Americans.

I often heard Mr and Mrs Kipling say hard things about America, but they had a great many American friends – my own relations the Drexels of Philadelphia among them. Kipling's attitude to the Americans reminded me of that of William Randolph Hearst to the English when I met him many years later in Hollywood. He was charming to me and his many other English friends, but he thoroughly disliked us as a nation.

The war ended, and as I then spent some time abroad it was two years before I revisited Bateman's. He was then at work on *The Irish Guards in the Great War,* a work of love. One line in it is more poignant than anything he ever wrote. It reads: '2nd Lieutenant Kipling was wounded and missing.'

He had been devoting a great deal of time to the War Graves Commission. His hatred of the Germans ('they are either at your feet or at your throat, old man') was deep-rooted, and he believed that it would not be long before England and France (that 'Mother of Swords' he loved so dearly) would be dragged into another war. In many ways he had become less tolerant. He was always an imperialist and a die-hard Tory, and he never forgave my old friend Oliver Baldwin, son of the prime minister who was Kipling's cousin, for sitting in the House of Commons as a socialist.

Kipling's work on the War Graves Commission had drawn him very close to King George V. One night I called at Brown's. He and Carrie had just returned from a dinner-party with 'the monarch'. When I asked him whether the king read books, he replied, dropping his voice to his dramatic whisper: 'No, old man, he reads men – volumes of 'em, sends for 'em, and they tell him the story.'

I knew from the twinkling blue eyes and the sing-song voice that he was delighted with his reply. By that time I was trying to make my own way as a writer, and my curiosity was no longer so easily appeased. I knew that the king could never send for Flaubert, Voltaire, Rabelais or Proust. I felt that George V's regard for Kipling, and the pleasure he took in his company,

D

was because of the writer's vast knowledge of 'the Services', even greater than that of the monarch himself.

The Government, however, was never able to persuade him to take an honour, and when Kipling received a letter from the prime minister's office informing him that he had been made a Companion of Honour. Mrs Kipling told me that his indignation was indescribable. It was not the honour that he despised so much as not being consulted about its acceptance.

'Supposing you had received a letter telling you that you had been made a bishop,' he wrote to Bonar Law, prime minister at the time, 'how would you have felt about it?' Bonar Law, quick to realise in what dangerous waters he was cruising, immediately withdrew the citation and all was well. There must, on this occasion, have been an error in some government department, as I have always understood that the recipient of a high honour is invited to accept it before it is bestowed.

One evening we were discussing South Africa long before the hideous policy of apartheid had been introduced. Kipling was sitting in front of the long bookshelf that ran the length of his study. It was a cold, miserable night, with the wind howling outside and the little river in flood. A fire was burning merrily in the hearth, but so vivid was his description of Rhodes's house that it was the sun of the African south that warmed me, not the winter fire, and it was not the Sussex logs that I smelled, but the sweet clinging perfume of eucalyptus. Cecil Rhodes had built a little cottage, known as 'The Woolsack', near his own big house, and this he had placed at the Kiplings' disposal whenever they wished. 'Rhodes,' said Kipling, 'stood head and shoulders above his contemporaries. He was the greatest man I ever met.' I asked him about Rhodes's close friend Jameson. 'The doctor and Rhodes were on different planes. There were certain things that fell into Rhodes's lap, but Jameson had to fight for everything.

'After the Raid he had to fight for it all over again.' He won. Greatly daring, I asked whether Jameson had been in his mind when he wrote 'If', but Kipling was always evasive when someone mentioned 'If'.

On the subject of Rhodes he was never tired of talking. He represented to Kipling the ideal being, a man of action with a dream, a man with an objective in life from which nothing but death was going to deflect him. 'I grant you that he could be ruthless in the acquisition of money. He had to be, old man. Money meant power, the power to realise his dream of driving a corridor bang through the vast African hinterland from the Cape to the gates of Cairo.'

One afternoon was taken up with a small alert Canadian who was writing a book on the Canadian Army, the first 50,000, who were fighting so gallantly in Flanders. It would have been impossible not to have marked him down as a man of destiny. Later I learned that his name was Max Aitken, one day to become the first and last Baron Beaverbrook.

About this time Kipling was writing the verse 'The Irish Guards', and he gave me the original manuscript.

I suggested that, as it was to be made into a song, Sir Edward Elgar might be invited to compose the music. 'No,' he said abruptly, 'Edward German will set my verses to music.' German's music was melodious and charming, but I was disappointed it was not to be Elgar – a great composer with a superb sense of pageantry – I said nothing because I had learned to keep my mouth shut whenever Carrie shot me one of her warning glances.

I would dearly have liked to know what Elgar had done to offend Kipling. The poet had written 'If' and wished to forget it; the musician had composed *Salut d'Amour* and, in turn, wished to forget it. Even in Victorian times 'a little fooling now and then was relished by the wise men'. But if Kipling was the leading poet of that period, Elgar was surely the leading composer.

It seemed to me that Kipling never had a story out of his head, and he would often try them out on me. He had a way of tossing you an idea which he expected you to treat as a dog treats a bone. I had recently begun writing adventure books, and had come back to England from New York with a gangster-thriller. On its publication I included it in a parcel of books I sent to Bateman's. By return of post, for he read at a prodigious speed, R.K. wrote:

Batemans, Burwash, Sussex.
January 29, 1923.

Dear Rupert,

Very many thanks for the generous packet of books, which will be especially welcome at Monte Carlo, where we hope to go almost at once, to meet George and Elsie. If you hear that bank is broke, you will know why.

I like Morley's 'Humble Fisherman' because he owns up to taking delight in small trout. That's a mark of sincerity. And he has a lovely touch.

Naturally, I read your book first. I don't suppose the facts are any less sickening than your fiction has made 'em, but it's about time to leave those people to themselves.

I don't care for their Invisible Exports in the film and murder line, which have done us morally about as much harm as cocaine. Can't you continue your two English characters, one of 'em anyhow, and cut him loose on a reform 'mission' of his own. Most of those Dago gents have an Italian record either politically, or frank carbonari, socially, haven't they? Some of 'em are wanted in Italy for conspiracy. What price your Englishman faking a super society (with the long arm of Mussolini's agents hinted at in the background) muscling-in on New York with nothing so vulgar as automatics, but poison. The old Lucrezia Borgia game. That would mean the big shots would have to use 'tasters'. You see the implication and developments. No need to use fatal poison. A stuff that brought a man out in spots and twisted his face aside would be enough to begin with. The Dago funk disease as few races do. Anyway, it would be a change of technique and might be made really quaint. You try, or get someone else to do it.

Our united love to you, and Good Luck

Ever sincerely,
R.K.

There is a South American preparation of coffee-root which is supposed to turn a man gaga for life in a few months. The mere rumour of that being loose in the underworld would produce splendid results.

One lovely summer day I decided to motor down to Bateman's. I took my old friend Patrick Kirwan with me. He had recently written *Black Exchange,* a brilliant book about Berlin life. Pat, when he was in the mood, behaved like a devil, but he wrote like an angel, so I knew that Kipling would enjoy meeting him. Kipling was in his best form and so, fortunately, was Pat. The old garden was smiling under a noonday sun when we arrived. Everything seemed very much the same. Mrs Kipling was a little older, with her funny nervous cough, her twinkling blue eyes and welcoming smile. Elsie was not there, for she had married George Bambridge, who was one of the most gallant and popular officers in the regiment, and they were living in Cambridge. Kipling, a little greyer, was still smoking out a cherrywood pipe a month. I had taken him down a tin of his special mixture from Philip Morris in Bond Street.

'Never smoke tobacco with Latakia in it, old man.'

As we walked out by the side door onto the lawn I noticed his great collection of odd walking-sticks was still being added to. He told Pat that during my convalescence he had found me asleep one night under a roof of his heavy leather-bound manuscripts. My explanation was that at that time I had discovered that I was walking in my sleep and I believed that if I had to move a great weight I would wake up. Recounting the story, Kipling would always say in conclusion 'and then I knew that for all the years of writing I hadn't laboured in vain'.

Kipling believed that a second world war was fast approaching and he had already advised Macmillan's and Methuen that none of his future books were to carry the imprint of the swastika, a Hindu fertility symbol 'swiped' from him by Hitler.

Now the day had come when for the last time I was to see those eyebrows raised and the grey-blue eyes opening wide in delight.

That afternoon he talked of everything from tuning a drum to the casting of the *Queen Mary*'s propellers – for he could talk with technical authority on almost any matter. 'I never forget anything I've been told, and I never forget anything I've read. It's all a question of memory, old man.'

No writer understood better the art and technique of writing. Every word should fit tight like a rivet in a bridge, and each rivet must be doing its job. Willie Somerset Maugham wrote of Kipling: 'He is our greatest story-writer. I can't believe he will ever be equalled, and I am sure that he will never be excelled.'

Kipling claimed that he had never published a story that in the original had not been twice as long. 'Cut and cut,' he advised, 'and when you've done that, cut again.' That afternoon of our last meeting, he turned to us. 'Writing is like fishing,' he said. 'You cast your hook into the stream, that's the story part; but you must first bait your hook; you must bait your hook with words.' His voice sank to that lovely stage-whisper, the mischievous look twinkled in his eyes: 'Gaudy words, old man, gaudy words.'

He came to the gate to see us off and spoke the last words I was to hear from his lips. 'I'll soon be having a bonfire for you to light, old man,' he said. And for the last time his hand, palm upwards, was thrust out at me.

He died in 1936. His friend, George V, lay desperately ill. It was said in the whispering capital that the king too must be dying; for his trumpeter had gone before him.

7

Faith in Flanders

ON 9 October 1917 I was back in France and the regiment was in action again. To reach our objective we had to cross the ill-omened Broembeek, a stream of water, now mostly mud, that incredibly persisted on its course through the shell-craters and the tortured desolation of the earth. We crossed this obstacle with remarkably few losses, though it was here we expected to meet the heaviest shelling. In the broken ground beyond it was a different story. Here were massively fortified positions, pill-boxes and a sandbagged strongpoint called Egypt House. Nests of machine-guns caught us in searing cross-fire as we stumbled forward from one position to another. Aeroplanes streaked low overhead, signalling back our movements and bringing heavy fire. Our gallant company commander, Bruce Reford, was wounded. At last we dug in as best we could just short of Houthulst Forest, under continuous fire from snipers on platforms in the splintered trees. It was here that Pat Ogilvy died. Pat, a dark, handsome Scot of the Bonnie House of Airlie, with laughing steel-grey eyes, was a man of indescribable charm. On this October day he moved into the telescopic sights of a German sniper, sitting high in a tree on the forest's edge. This enemy stranger increased the pressure on the trigger and the bullet tore into Pat's body. He fell with no words, only a long-drawn sigh. Pat, who was a lovely man, must certainly be walking as an equal with the gods and the poets in Valhalla.

On this day and the three following we lost 4 officers killed and 7 wounded, 48 other ranks killed and 158 wounded, with 10 missing either through direct hits or drowned in the sea of

mud. This was officially described as 'a successful minor operation'. We had gained maybe a few hundred yards of sodden,
useless soil.

In a brief lull that followed the attack, kneeling before our
chaplain, Father du Moulin Browne, I made my confession and
was received into the Roman Catholic Church.

Like many Irish Guards Officers, Protestant or otherwise, I
always went in command of my men to their church parade and
attended their Mass. I never failed to be strangely moved by the
simple devotion of these hard-bitten Irish soldiers to the rites of
their ancient faith. Accoutred for war, they knelt bare-headed in
sun, wind or rain before their priest at his improvised altar and
told their beads, the whisper of the battle that awaited them
echoing their own muttered 'Our Fathers' and 'Hail Marys'.

The seeds of my own late-ripening faith had already been
sown in the great cathedrals of France and Italy. Thus, slowly,
I had fallen in love with the Church as a man falls in love with a
woman; but my love was a secret love, for I usually had Father
with me and Father believed sincerely in an English Protestant
god whom I thought of as being rather like himself: majestic and
powerful, but not quite so indulgent towards his children.

The discipline of the Church I was prepared to accept: after
the brigade that would not be difficult. The Articles of Faith
pointed, without short-cuts, the way that led to God, and it was a
way I wished to follow; but it was the mystical romance of the
liturgy, the fragrant reek of the incense eddying heavenwards
with my prayers and the all-pervading ambiance of worship,
faith and beauty that held me to my secret purpose.

I received no formal 'instruction': in the vast areas of France
and Flanders death was too busy on its day-and-night assignment
to allow those of the 'Shining order of Melchizedek' much time
to spare for other than the immediate victims. Moreover, this
activity, as I saw it, lent a certain urgency to the matter; and so
my secret resolve was accomplished kneeling in the peaceful
twilight of a priest's tent to the distant and interminable rumble
of the guns.

I survived the next tour of duty unscathed until the night of the 14th, when a shell burst in a near-by crater and a lump of shrapnel got me in the leg just above the ankle. I was carried for six hours over miles of slippery duckboards where one wrong step by a stretcher-bearer would have toppled all into the slimy sea about us to be sunk without trace in choking death. I lay looking up at the fading stars, drifting between sleeping and waking, until I felt a gentle pressure on my wrist and one of the great-hearted bearers told me I was at the dressing-station. The medical officer, after examining me, gave me the choice of having my foot off straightaway or risking the onset of gangrene on the journey to hospital and the consequent removal of my leg above the knee.

I chose to take the risk; so he extracted as much metal as he could find and sewed tubes in the wound to drain it; then I was put on a train for the Base. Somewhere in the night it stopped, and through a veil of sleep and anaesthesia I heard another train crawl alongside, coming to a halt with each wagon crashing against the other in a long series of receding bangs. These were sounds recognised, comforting and welcome. We had arrived at Étaples. I spent ten days at the Duchess of Westminster's Hospital (in the Casino in Le Touquet), where I was operated on and then dispatched, with a label describing my wound tied on my pyjamas, to the American Women's Hospital in London. My leg and foot were still intact.

This hospital happened to be, conveniently, next door to our London home at 100 Lancaster Gate. In spite of this, or because of it, Mother wanted to make a hole through the party wall so that I could be passed through on a stretcher as soon as I was well enough to spend the day with her and the family. She even called in a builder to survey the job. Finally, Lady Randolph Churchill, Winston's mother, who was in charge, persuaded her that it was a little impractical, as the labour of carrying me out of one front-door into the next was less complicated than embarking on structural alterations to the dividing wall between them.

One day a V.A.D. collected a tray I had been nursing on my knees the whole morning. 'I'm glad you've come for it,' I said, 'I was getting *très fatigué*.'

D2

'You must be getting well to make such an atrocious pun,' she said, smiling.

I woke one morning to find my future brother-in-law Dick Rawlinson in the next bed to mine. He was in the Intelligence Corps, but there was no mystery about his presence. Apparently they had discovered a needle in one of his feet and he had come in to have it extracted before it started on its travels.

Although I had been twice operated on successfully I felt bound to warn him that if he had any say in the selection of surgeon he should avoid the one who saturated the atmosphere in which he moved with the strong reek of Scotch whisky. Without a word being said, Dick quietly dressed in the dim light and, with a friendly nod to me, left the ward. As far as I know the needle is in his person to this day, but I was much impressed with the way, having come to a decision, he put it into immediate operation.

Soon after, I was myself allowed out on crutches. At that time the only crutches in England were heavy timber jobs that supported their user by the armpits. Lord Leopold Mountbatten, with his usual thoughtfulness, sent to Paris for a pair of the type in use in France, which support from the forearm. He presented them to me one day in Well's Club, which was always known as Swears. It was above Atkinson's in Old Bond Street and was the meeting-place of the *jeunesse dorée*, drawn largely from the sporting and gambling section of the Brigade of Guards and the Green Jackets. A few weeks later, after a pint of champagne, I felt so well and confident on my feet that I gave my crutches to a wounded man who was providentially standing on the corner by Atkinson's. I walked a little way unsteadily, then hailed a taxi; but I never went back to crutches.

Soon afterwards I received a letter from Sir Courteney Forbes. I later met him many times, particularly when he was Ambassador in Lima, but at that time, though we had had friends in common, we had met only casually. He invited me to dine, and I was surprised when I arrived at the St James's Club to find I was the sole guest. I knew, vaguely, that he was employed at the Foreign Office, but it was the first time I had talked to him, and he impressed me vastly. After he had ordered dinner (with a perfect Chambertin) he told me that it had been arranged for me to carry a diplomatic bag to Rome as a temporary King's Messenger.

As soon as I was able to walk without crutches, Aunt Maude Valérie White had given me a letter of introduction to Sir Eyre Crowe, Under-Secretary of State for Foreign Affairs. I had enquired about the possibility of being employed during my convalescence. He had suggested that I should write to Sir Godfrey Thomas, Head of Communications, which I had done, and this presumably was the outcome.

Courteney then proceeded to tell me something of the history of the corps and what was expected of me. Since the time of Charles II, when the Corps of King's and Queen's Foreign Service Messengers was formed, the Messengers have served their Sovereigns 'by carrying out their sacred duties to preserve, secure and inviolate, to the utmost of their power, under every circumstance and every emergency, the dispatches entrusted to their care'.

When Charles was in exile on the Continent, he instituted a regular service of messengers to convey his letters to England from Holland and back. In most cases the messengers were skippers of Dutch fishing-smacks and, as few of them could speak English, it was necessary to provide them with a means of ensuring safe delivery.

Charles had with him at the time a silver dish on the lid of which were embossed four greyhounds. These he cut off, two he gave to his Dutch Messenger and two to his English contact, so that on meeting at a certain tavern in Dover they were able to identify themselves. When Charles regained the throne he decreed that the silver greyhound should be worn with the blue ribbon of the Order of the Garter. From then on this became the official badge of the corps.

The number of Messengers, Courteney explained, has varied with the exigencies of the time. Each Messenger has to be prepared to leave for the utmost ends of the world at literally an hour's notice. Once they travelled by horse-post, by post-chaise and packet-boat.

'Now you travel by car and by air, by H.M. ships and, sometimes, by ocean-liner. Secret dispatches are carried by Messenger because the essence of the contract is not so much speed as security. The contents of the cross-labelled canvas bags are mostly top-secret communications between the Foreign Office in Whitehall and His Britannic Majesty's Ambassadors and representatives abroad.'

The corps, he told me, was never likely to be supplanted by any other method of communication where top secrets were concerned, because the air could be tapped too freely, messages unscrambled, ciphers broken, and because decoding had reached so high a level of efficiency that there was no cipher that could not, eventually, be broken down.

The King's Messenger was never parted from his bags and the pouch in which he carried certain special letters. They were always with him, from the time he received the way-bill until he reached his destination, where he obtained a receipt. Thus there was no possibility of the contents of a bag being extracted, photographed, replaced and the bag resealed. Out of a King's Messenger's sight and possession, even for a few minutes, a bag would be compromised.

'The closest security measures are observed in all journeys,' Courteney explained. 'Cars, railway-carriages and cabins are reserved *en route*; and a Messenger is given special facilities for passing through customs and passport barriers. The trust placed in a Messenger by our department is implicit. It is left entirely to your discretion to decide with whom you may wish to pass your time during a journey. You are responsible to no one except your chief in London, and there are no rules laid down to guide you. You must understand, therefore, that we expect the King's Messenger to be a man of unusual character and resource. By the very nature of your employment you must possess a breadth of outlook and the necessary charm to smooth things over when obstacles arise *en voyage*, and you have to command the respect of foreign officials with whom you'll come in contact. In short, you should be as much at home in an *auberge* in Provence as you are at an ambassador's table. In the Foreign Office you will see hanging on the wall a motto adopted by the corps: a quotation from Herodotus: 'Neither snow nor rain nor heat nor gloom of night shall stay these couriers in the swift completion of their appointed rounds.'

Courteney leaned back. He had done his job of indoctrination: 'I think a glass of Cockburn's '97 might be a good idea.'

To describe my feelings as elated would be an understatement. Even if I was to make only this one journey as King's Messenger before rejoining the regiment I was making my first contact with the corps. That night when I left the St James's Club I floated down Piccadilly. It was my first experience, too, of levitation. I gather I am one of the privileged few to have enjoyed this most delightful form of movement several times in the course of life. I know of nothing comparable. You are never divorced from the earth, as when travelling in an aircraft; you are still part of the procession of life; but you have the wonderful bird-like advantage of watching from above the movements of the mere mortals below.

I levelled off somewhere near Hyde Park Barracks, coming to earth at Rutland Gate, when I completed the short journey home on foot.

8

Roman Holiday

My journey as a King's Messenger in that hot summer of 1918 was, to my disappointment, most uneventful. At the Embassy in Rome, in the absence of the Archivist, I handed my 'crossed' bag to Captain MacGregor Whitton, the young military attaché, who looked exactly as all military attachés should look: handsome, intelligent and soldierly. He at once informed me I would be expected for dinner at the Embassy.

In conversation later he told me that Father was in Rome. At that time Father was Director of Ship Repairs (Foreign) with offices in the Admiralty, Paris and Rome. I knew that he made the Excelsior his headquarters, so I booked in at the Grand. It was not that I wanted to avoid him, but I felt that first I must explore Rome on my own. I wanted to see the Eternal City through my own eyes and had no wish to be raised to the level of a student and put through an historical and archaeological course. When in Rome do as the Romans. I had more than a vague idea what they did; now was my opportunity to learn exactly how they did it. To be truthful, what I wanted was a dark-eyed Roman girl with eyelids painted green, who would lead me to a flower-shop and thence to a café where we would spend the day drinking ice-cold wine; and in the evening make pilgrimage to Keats's grave. That was my idea of a day in Rome. I had, therefore, to keep out of Father's way. I had still to learn that life is rarely as simple as one would wish, so it came as a blow when I found him among the guests in the Embassy drawing-room.

Sir James Rennell Rodd, the Ambassador, was a man of immense charm; it was said of him that even his dreams were in Latin and Greek. He was one of the old school of cultured diplomats and he probably knew Rome better than the Romans. He had been posted there as attaché in his youth and had served on there as First Secretary, Counsellor and, finally, Ambassador.

He was loved by the Italians, but in Roman society Lady Rodd could be remarkably outspoken when it pleased her to be; in consequence they were frequently referred to as Sir Rennell Rodd and Lady Rude.

At dinner that evening he told us that he never walked in Rome without seeing something beautiful he had not previously observed. As he said this, I caught Father's eye and I knew that he was already planning where he would take me the following day; and that would be the end of my dream of the dark-eyed Roman girl. Nor was I mistaken, for when I dropped him off later at the Excelsior he made me promise I would report the following morning.

That night at the Grand Hotel I found a member of Father's staff waiting for me. He was determined that I should see some Roman night-life, and it is only fair to say that he had little difficulty in persuading me. He was a brilliant linguist. To mystify people, especially those who fancied themselves as linguists, he would mix languages. First, he would speak Italian with a German accent, then he would switch to German with a Swedish accent or Polish with a Greek accent. People seldom identified his true nationality.

There were moments when he displayed a burning zest for living; and others when it was as if he was annoyed at being a member of the human race. He spoke about himself with brilliant introspection, which was not surprising, as it was the subject in which he was most interested. I found him instructive rather than entertaining, but such was my yearning for worldly information that I was most content to be in his company, for I realised he was a man with considerable knowledge to impart.

He invariably carried a Malacca cane, crowned with a round ivory knob, exquisitely carved in the shape of a lion's head. He wielded this beautiful object accurately and unmercifully in the pursuit of cats, creatures he loathed with a cold hatred, as unsavoury as his dislike for anyone Jewish. Returning from a tour of bordellos and cafés in the early hours of a lovely Roman dawn, his searching eyes detected a cat crouched in the shadow. His cane flashed and there was a sharp crack. The animal's skull slowly opened and the brains blossomed and then seedily spilled like the outpouring of an overripe melon.

Because of my wound I was still too weak to assail him physically, and his logic outmatched mine. Had I told Father of the extra-mural activities of 'the cat-hunter', he would at once have arranged his transfer elsewhere, for Father was essentially humane and he would have regarded him as a man with blood on his hands. My own attitude was one of disgust weakened, as usual, by indecision. I sought to persuade myself that it was the duty of every cat to exercise its self-protective instinct at the approach of danger; for I cannot think that anything as decisive as death is not preceded by some hitherto unclassified smell, which animals, with their sharp premonitory instincts, should be the first to recognise. I have always disliked a guttering candle, nor will I snuff one out, not because it is a symbolical gesture, but because I detest the blue smoke as it snakes up to the ceiling followed, as thunder follows lightning, by the stench of decay, its musty fumes all-enveloping and entombing. Could not a similar necrophiliac breath be the precursor of death as the shadow of destiny closes in on us?

If I informed on 'the cat-hunter' I knew that Father would lose a first-class negotiator. Was it for me to weigh in the balance the importance of the work that he was doing against the lives of a few stray cats? We were living in times when death had ceased to surprise, though it could still shock. Judged in the light of those days he might have been better employed in killing Germans, to which no stigma was attached, but killing cats was still considered inhuman and ungentlemanly. On reflection, he might have used this distasteful talent more profitably in the Ypres salient, which I had only recently left.

There, in no-man's-land, the territory between our trenches

and the enemy's had become the hunting-ground of an army of animals. When we were on night-patrol they would streak silently away as we surprised them. In the grey dawn these creatures of the night would emerge in the shape of fat, contented cats, with their mouths and whiskers glazed from their latest meal, devoured in some fresh crater that the stretcher-bearers had not cleared; or snatched from a body crucified on the wire or draped over the barbs like the letter U. During these fat years the cats and rats lived in amity, so rich was the feast.

The last time I saw him was on a grey afternoon in a London club. He was crouched in an armchair, and by some strange trick of lighting his face had assumed the mask of a cat, plump and content.

The only other creature I have met akin to him was an Austrian friend of my sister Ailsa and her husband, Dick Rawlinson, whom I met at their home in Sussex. I felt vaguely disturbed by him, and when I examined him more closely I observed that there was a certain animal expression about his eyes and that his teeth were pointed like those of a wolf. When he left I mentioned this to them and they laughed my ideas off as absurd; the man was a successful businessman and a first-class golfer.

A few months later I was in Sussex again and I heard Dick say to his little boy, Peter (now the distinguished lawyer and politician, Sir Peter), 'Go and tidy yourself before Mr X comes.' Whereupon Peter replied, 'Oh, Daddy, I don't like him at all. When he kisses me he always bites my neck.'

I believe that there must be truth in a legend as persistent as that of the werewolf, and nothing will convince me that there is not.

I spent the next day in Rome at the disposition of Father and, I might say devoutly, of God, because we visited at least ten of the Eternal City's six hundred churches. Each seemed to me more beautiful and moving than the one before. We held our tapers surrounded by a group of camphor-smelling nuns in the musty darkness of the catacombs, into which, with my un-confessed hangover, I had been drawn so reluctantly. Later we

descended the Spanish Steps and lunched on *pasta* and drank
Chianti in a restaurant under a cool awning to the music of a
fountain. When I became impatient (because I still wanted to
meet the dark-eyed Roman girl) Father said: 'Never hurry a
waiter; a waiter never hurries you.'

Afterwards we walked in the Borghese gardens, but it was in
one of the more secret gardens whose dusty paths deadened the
sound of our feet, in the deep shade and resinous scent of a line
of cypresses that Father said: 'Rome is like drinking a good wine;
so far you've only had a sip of it.'

In those days the Colosseum was a mass of scarlet weeds
sprung from the blood of pagan lions and Christian martyrs; and
the Palatine was the home of blue irises. The mountainous ruins
of the Baths of Caracalla were covered in moss and fern; and
only the arches, dizzily suspended in the Roman sky, were bare
and polished. That summer's day Rome was a city of wild
flowers and dark-eyed girls and a thousand fountains.

It had been a long and lovely day. We had wandered through
the palaces and gazed at pictures, tapestries and painted ceilings.
We had lingered beside dancing and cascading waters, which
Father must have seen many times, but he was never tired of
opening my eyes to new and exquisite things. I asked him how
they had raised the many tall obelisks I had seen and he replied
rather vaguely: 'With ropes and pulleys and the sweat of slaves
watched by a silent motionless populace. You see, there was one
penalty only for making a sound or disturbing the air when they
were raising an obelisk, and that was death.'

Years later I visited the city, but it was without his tall,
upright figure beside me, and no one turned to look as they did
when he was there. We drove back to the Excelsior as dusk fell
on the city. I drank a cocktail in the sitting-room while he
changed for dinner. We were not to dine together; he had other
arrangements. For all I know he, not I, was dining with the
dark-eyed Roman girl, with her eyelids painted green, and they
would drink ice-cold wine in the flower-shop and never give a
thought to poor Keats.

Father knew that I was on my way somewhere, that my mission

was at an end and I was due to report to the regiment; but I had not been prepared to tell him where, though he had asked me. All he said was: 'When I'm uncertain where I'm going I invariably have my bags packed for Paris and I usually find I unpack them at the Crillon.' He spoke rather dryly, though his eyes were smiling

I can see him now, magnificent in his dinner-jacket, with the scarlet rosette of the *Légion d'honneur* in his buttonhole, his linen smelling faintly of *fougère royale* and his brown face smiling. 'No one ever tells me anything ...', he paused thoughtfully, '... unless they're in trouble.'

He was right in his guess that I would unpack my bag in Paris; but I had no intention of going there direct. In fact I had already booked a *wagon-lit* compartment on the train to Monte Carlo. I travelled through the night with the window open to let in the smell of eucalyptus and pine and cedar.

Everyone has a place of dreams to which he must go or to which he wishes to return; but we learn as we grow older that it is to what we remember that we wish to return. And, alas, nothing can ever be as we remember it, and we too have changed. I had been in Monte Carlo as a boy only, with my mother and father. Now I was to return alone as a man.

Next morning I left the train at the station before Monte Carlo. I had told the *wagon-lit* attendant to put my bag off at Monte Carlo. I wanted to approach the principality on foot.

The colour and shape of flowers have never ceased to amaze me, but unfortunately I can name very few. Old James was our grandparents' coachman, and when grandfather died and father inherited High Meadow he inherited Old James with the house and stables. When motor cars came in, the horses and carriages went out, and there was no job for the old man. In spite of the fact that he knew nothing about flowers or gardens, father appointed him head gardener, remarking blithely, 'He'll soon learn'; which was a little optimistic as Old James was then about eighty. Wearing a large straw sombrero he wandered abroad, prodding anything that looked like a weed and chatting with the nurses as he lit and relit his old pipe. Often I would walk with him, for apart from his gentleness to me – he loved children – his long white beard never ceased to fascinate me.

It was under his instruction that I learned the names of flowers. Unfortunately, rather than display his ignorance, he taught me names of flowers and trees born of his imagination, and I have been ignorant on the subject ever since, apart from orchids, carnations, roses and the other flowers one sends to girls. I believe James enjoyed my childish company because I was an attentive audience for his picturesque invective against the motor car, which he hated with a fierce hatred. It was probably my first realisation of the verb 'to hate'. I can never forget the expression of scorn that crowned his words when he spoke of that part of his stables which had been converted into a garage; a foreign word that he refused to use, referring to it contemptuously as the 'garry-house'. Though the under-gardeners must have realised how little he knew, they were too overawed by his patriarchal figure to argue with him. What wonderful names he could have invented for the vivid flowers of Monaco.

The morning was brilliant as I set off along the Corniche. I could see in the distance, silhouetted against the blue sea, the white towers of the Casino, the curved façade of the Hôtel de Paris and, on a lower level, the oriental domes of the Café de Paris. The air was fragrant with verbena. Bougainvillea splashed in cascades of purple, pink and deep-red over the walls of villas and hotels. In the Rue des Moulins the shops were just opening and, suddenly, I was walking in the cool shadows cast by striped awnings.

I bought a box of Roger et Gallet carnation soap, the loveliest of all soaps, whose fragrance can take its place with the great smells of the world: Havana tobacco, mimosa and well-cured leather. For me it will always be associated with this visit to Monte Carlo, just as the haunting melodies of *Prince Igor* will always recall Moscow.

The season at Monte Carlo in those days was from February to the end of April. The Hôtel de Paris was open all the year round and so was the Casino. I had been given a letter to Monsieur Fleurie, the director of the hotel. This exquisitely groomed and bearded man must have assumed that because I was visiting Monte Carlo in July I was either mad or a poet; and as madmen and poets walk with kings and princes, he gave me the royal suite for the price of a double bedroom.

It was Monte Carlo in war-time, but the Germans were a long way from Monaco and most of the residents were still there, many of them having turned their villas into nursing-homes for convalescent officers. There was a large colony of Russian refugees who had escaped from the Bolsheviks and clustered in villas near the Grand Duke Michael.

That night I went into the Casino for the first time. I had changed into plain clothes as no one in uniform was admitted. The Casino has always reserved the right to refuse entrance to anyone on any pretext. When Frank Otter, a friend of mine, who lived on nothing more solid than the driest champagne, was refused admittance, it was not because his trousers were turned up, but because he had forgotten to put on shoes and socks.

Monte Carlo, even in those war days and in the years to follow when I came to know and love it, was a unique place. The Casino was the only one (other than San Remo and Ostend) where roulette was played. People staying in the principality might possibly visit Cannes, Nice or Mentone during their stay; but those at the other Riviera towns visited Monte Carlo at least once a week. On Father's first visit, in the eighties, the principality still had an *octroi* and he complained bitterly when he was made to pay duty on a tennis racquet, as he was unable to convince the customs men that it was not a musical instrument.

The currency was the gold louis, and the croupiers, who were allowed no pockets in their clothes, were rewarded for services by having the *pourboire* slipped down their collars, which they wore large and loose.

The prince, a famous naturalist, lived aboard his yacht, a floating aquarium, but Camille Blanc, the Casino's chief concessionaire, was the real king of Monte Carlo. Father once asked him whether the Casino had enjoyed a good season, whereupon Camille Blanc replied: 'Rouge gagne et noir gagne mais Blanc gagne toujours.'

The Casino engaged the world's leading opera singers. It was here, as a small boy, that I heard Caruso and Melba as Rodolfo and Mimi. Caruso's noble, metallic tenor was probably too powerful for the beautiful little theatre; strong odours of garlic filled the air. It was one of the seven wonders of the opera world that Melba was able to sing with him so gloriously without being gassed. In addition he delighted in whispering dirty stories to her during her death scene.

Diaghilev, a streak of white like a plume in his black hair, formed his first successful ballet company there with Nijinsky, Karsavina, Mordkin and Pavlova.

Monte Carlo was a gambling centre, but it was also the cultural capital of the Côte d'Azur. The Hôtel de Paris, with its magnificent tapestries, rugs and Empire furniture, was then one of the most beautiful hotels in the world. It is no longer so. Today the visitor is more likely to see pin-tables and tubular chairs where *buhl* cabinets and Louis XVI sofas and chairs once stood. Ciro's, in the gallery behind the Café de Paris, was one of a small but exquisite chain of international restaurants that sustained the world of fashion in Paris, Deauville and the Pyrenean Luchon, with an exclusive club of the same name in London.

The standard of cooking was *cordon bleu*, the wines, cigars and service of a quality rarely obtainable today. In all Ciro's restaurants the décor was the same: Persian rugs on marble floors, French panelled rooms, star-studded mirrors with crystal chandelier lighting. Fabulous sums of money were spent on flowers, and the whole cigar-and-tuberose-scented atmosphere was one of unhurried ease. Time meant little and money was solely for spending.

There were no casual sports clothes as we know them now. The crease in a man's trousers was a matter of prime importance. His brown-and-white buckskin shoes were made at Peal's or Lobb's in London, or Grégoire in Paris; his suits by Scholte or Johns & Pegg; his ties in Jermyn Street or the Rue de Castiglione; cigarettes – Pera, Balkan Sobranie or Boguslavsky – were as often as not taken from a Fabergé case with a speckled silk tinder-cord.

At night the male front-studs, cabochon sapphire and diamonds, and onyx and diamond cuff-links rivalled the women's jewels. It was the high season of archdukes, American millionaires and their lovely children, wealthy *émigré* Russians and the faithful pleasure-loving English.

For whose benefit did they all dress up? Ornithologists have suggested that the female bird remains indifferent to the brilliant plumage of the male. Did the Edwardian and post-war dandies, like the Georgian beaux, dress more for the mirror than for the female? Beau Brummell was the first of the dandies to advocate cleanliness instead of overpowering the human exhalations with perfume. Brummel said: 'A gentleman's linen should smell but of the open', and preached the evangel of simplicity in all things. But in the time of my youth a man of fashion, less faithful to his austere creed, would rarely take under a couple of hours to bath and dress. This, of course, with the help of his manservant.

The bath-water would be at the correct temperature and lightly redolent of verbena; the shaving soap, probably Roger et Gallet's 'Violette', smoothly foaming on the badger brush; the eau-de-toilette to hand, on the shelf beneath the mirror Atkinson's eau-de-Cologne, *peau d'Espagne, fougère royale*, or one of Penhaligon's perfumes, made up in Jermyn Street for men only. In the bath the large cake of soap would come from Morny's, the ample sponge from the Levant, and the loofah from the Barbary Coast. Thus cleansed and refreshed the man of fashion would be dried in Turkish towels and later, in the dressing-room, helped into his silken vest and underpants. He would then make a decision on socks to match the suit he had chosen. Next for selection the shirt: white linen, tailored by Beale & Inman, or one of the shirtmakers of the Burlington Arcade, Jermyn Street. He would then seat himself to put on his socks. This accomplished, he would be assisted into his trousers, which were narrow and, before 1914, without turn-ups.

Now the shoes were laced and knotted by the manservant; or the buckskin-topped boots were pearl-buttoned, according to where he was staying. In Monte Carlo, Deauville, Cannes, Biarritz, Carlsbad and Marienbad in season it would, of course be brown leather and white buckskin – known later as co-respondent shoes. First one foot was thrust forward to the waiting shoe and shoe-horn, then the other. All this had the dignity and tempo of the minuet. Each partner in the rite knew just how much service in one case and help in the other was necessary to complete the perfect whole.

One trouser-leg and then the other was pulled neatly down over the socks and boots by the man. The master then stood up, holding his trousers by the waist, and turned his back to his man, who by that time had attached the braces to the back-buttons. All he had to do now was to throw them over his master's shoulders, who then buttoned them on, surveying himself the while in the long cheval-glass.

Several ties would have been laid out from which to make a choice. If he were wearing a pearl tie-pin then his tie could only be dark blue, never any other colour. The ties would bear the names Huskinson, Turnbull & Asser or Charvet. His suit might have been built (an Edwardian expression) at Poole's, King Edward VII's tailor.

At a royal garden party, to which Poole had been invited (for the king seldom paid him), he pushed himself forward and the monarch asked whether he was enjoying himself. 'Very much, sir, but isn't the company a little mixed?' he replied.

'Damn it all, Mr Poole,' said His Majesty, 'you can't expect us all to be tailors.'

Poole certainly made Savile Row famous throughout the world; but neither King Edward VII nor George V as Prince of Wales was ever able to popularise his practical notion of sewing the trouser-crease down the side.

By now our master has selected his tie and knotted it. His manservant stands by with a lavender waistcoat, linen in the summer, or the small linen slip to be worn inside the dark waistcoat and to be revealed as a glimpse of white along the edges of the vee. Nothing remains now but to put on the coat, into which he is deftly inserted. The man arranges the Irish linen handkerchief in the breast-pocket and affixes the flower in the buttonhole. Never must the flower betray foliage. A last survey in the cheval and, with Malacca cane and homburg hat, the man of fashion is ready to saunter out to the Croisette in Cannes or the Terrace in Monte Carlo.

I remember once a newly engaged man of mine asking me what clothes I intended wearing that day. I told him that I would be going to Lord's for the Eton and Harrow match. When I came out of the bath-room I was delighted and flattered to see, beautifully arranged on the suit-carrier, a white flannel shirt and trousers, white socks and co-respondent shoes; and the whole surmounted by a carefully balanced straw hat with a Brigade of Guards ribbon.

An Austrian friend, von Sparlein, had a manservant he had recruited from a Roumanian circus where Sparlie was pursuing a beautiful trapeze-artist. This man, Antoine, had a startling routine, which I witnessed several times. When Sparlie had been out riding in the Prater or the Tiergarten, Antoine would be waiting to divest him of his top-boots. Sparlie would seat himself, while Antoine would turn his backside to him and, bending astride the outstretched leg, take a firm grip on one of the heels. Then came the exactly calculated tug. To help him, Sparlie would put his other foot on the man's buttock and thrust. This in itself is, as we all know, a routine method of getting extracted from a top-boot, but Antoine's embellishment was what made the whole thing fabulous.

As he tugged and Sparlie pushed, the boot was released and at the precise moment of separation Antoine leapt into the air, doing a double-somersault that landed him in the exact position to remove the second boot. It was an acrobatic trick that called for perfect split-second timing between the partners.

Only once did I see the routine come unstuck and Antoine bang his head against the wall; but that was because he had failed to obtain opera seats for his master and Sparlie was in no mood to co-operate.

It is easily understandable how well master and man came to know each other in those days. They actually spent more time together than they did with their respective families. Turner was always able to tell us the best moment to approach Father when we wanted anything. Once, when Father was annoyed with his directors in Grayson, Rollo in Liverpool, he said to me: 'If I have any more trouble with them I'll appoint Turner managing director.'

They say that no man is ever a hero to his valet, but I know that Turner was often terrified of Father. The bond between master and man must be an instinctive one, each knowing when to give and when to take. It must have been a most unhappy relationship between Ernest Augustus, Duke of Cumberland and his valet in St James's Palace, for according to the official account the valet almost succeeded in murdering the Duke, while the unofficial rumour was that the Duke had murdered the valet. Most evidently one or other of the contracting parties fell very short of the ideals that the relationship demands; one that is fast passing from a world where there are no longer masters and men, but only managements and men.

9

Dulce est Desipere in Loco

THE war to end wars had ended, and with it my career as a soldier and temporary King's Messenger. Many years were to pass before again I was to start my travels in sealed compartments in the company of 'crossed' bags.

I had entered the war as a stripling; now I was a man – a man of leisure. So I enjoyed those years that followed, I ate well and drank deep, I played most of the kissing-games, both indoor and outdoor, in hotels and flats and country houses, on trains and yachts and on one occasion I must confess on a tombstone in the graveyard of a thirteenth-century church in Bangor, Caernarvonshire.[1] I mixed tolerably well with the café society of those days and nights. I went racing by day and, to parties at night, and I survived. I still called on the service of Turner whenever it was available, for Turner was more than a father, he was a major-domo, he was a friend and, what was very convenient, he was a banker. He seemed to carry a limitless supply of money at all times on his portly person.

I was down at Epsom one day, and I happened to be in the paddock, where, I am firmly convinced, the horses decide among themselves which is to win, when I noticed a lovely little filly called Pretty Girl dancing round, and as I was walking with a beautiful girl on my arm, I placed a £20 bet at 35 to 1 with Ladbroke's. Pretty Girl, the little outsider, waltzed home, winning by a lovely head. Next morning I decided to go over to Paris, and Turner without the blink of an eye advanced me £500 out of his hip pocket. He was that sort of butler.

[1] Not to be confused with Bangor, Northern Ireland.

I had acquired a habit, much appreciated by my friends, of having wine from Father's cellar sent to the restaurant where we were to dine, for he kept an excellent cellar. It was a pleasant surprise for my guests to see Turner, instead of the *sommelier*, pouring out the first glass with majestic indifference to the restaurant staff. Outside, ex-guardsman Cumberland, Mother's chauffeur, would be waiting in the Daimler to drive him to whichever rendezvous they might have arranged; for they were both what, at that time, was known as 'ladies' men'.

There was probably a heavy price in corkage charged to my account, but in those days credit flowed as freely as the wine and all the other things that go with it; for in the pursuit of pleasure I can honestly say that I never spared myself.

My expenditure at this period was far in excess of the generous allowance Father made me, but my credit was good and my tailor's, Johns & Pegg, were always good for a few hundred when I was pressed for ready cash. My heaviest accounts were a string of bars, cabarets and flower-shops in London and Paris; and Ladbroke's the commission agents with whom I had a running account. It was a way of life that might have continued had I not lavished money on a series of romantic affairs with young apprentice mistresses, from which I obtained little satisfaction except that which one feels when one has made oneself loved, if only fleetingly.

It was Turner who met me off the boat at Dover with a suitcase of clothes one grey Monday. It happened that on the preceding Saturday evening I had been on my way to a supper-party. *En route* I had stopped at Victoria Station to see friends off on the night-train to Paris. I had drunk no more than usual, but my friends were in hilarious form. My comparatively sober appearance in top-hat, white tie and tail-coat must have been too much for them, and as the train drew out of the station, as if by common instinct, they set upon me and I found myself Shanghaied aboard the train. Before we reached Folkstone I was delighted with what they had done.

Next morning at the Gare St-Lazare in my tail-coat, I was of considerable interest to sober Parisian commuters already going about their business. I was fortunate in that I already had shirts and socks in Paris, because in those days I used to send my laundry to Madame Blandier, a *blanchisseuse,* who returned it to London the following week exquisitely washed and smelling faintly of chestnuts. On this occasion I presented myself, without delay, at her apartment in the Rue de Passy. I knew that I was not only feeling the worse for wear, but also looking it after my overnight journey, so I had taken the precaution of carrying as many carnations as I could hold, for I knew they would do double duty by screening my wilting shirt and delighting the old lady.

She had, fortunately, not dispatched my fresh linen to London, so after I had changed into a clean shirt, tie and waistcoat, we went to the corner café where she drank a Vermouth-cassis to every *fine à l'eau* that I swigged down.

I spent a delightful week-end, remaining in bed at the Daunou during the day, giving instructions that I be called only in time to go out at night, to accord with the limits of my wardrobe.

The Hôtel Daunou at that time was a delightful *garçonnière,* immediately above Ciro's, and contained about thirty rooms, each with a bathroom, all occupied by such people as had no objection to the orchestra and dance-band from below, which played into the early hours of each morning. The only meal served was the morning *petit-déjeuner.*

The hotel was owned by Clement Hobson, who also had Ciro's and at one time had been involved in a murder case in Scotland. He was in due course acquitted under the third finding possible in Scottish law: 'Not Proven'. But for this enlightened jury I might never have found so pleasant a home in Paris.

My own first brush with law in Paris occurred about this time. Fortunately the incident ended happily, but among other things it taught me to avoid the company of police as assiduously as I had avoided that of masters at my schools.

I was visiting friends at the Meurice, that aristocrat among hotels. I stepped into the lift, minding my own business, as the

expression goes, when I was immediately confronted by the
only other occupant – a *gendarme* in uniform, wearing an eye-
glass, of all things. Believing that he was a guest attending a
fancy-dress party, I at once congratulated him on the originality
and accuracy of his get-up. To my amazement he became most
indignant and demanded an immediate apology. Seeing him
feeling for his note-book in an unmistakably official manner,
I was not slow in expressing my regrets and we parted amicably
after he had had a drink in my friends' suite.

This monstrous encounter taught me that I should always be
prepared for the unexpected, and that when I was clearly in
the wrong I should always be prepared to make felicitous
amends.

Years later I was to enter the same exclusive hotel by the
Rue de Rivoli entrance. A small group of men was standing
outside this same lift in a semicircle. I was about to pass through
the small *entresol* when the lift-door opened and Alfonso XIII,
King of Spain, stepped out. He gave his hand to each man in
the group which now included me. He obviously assumed that
I was one of the welcoming committee.

After his abdication in 1931 he frequently visited the Duke of
Sutherland at Sutton Place. Mother was living at that time in
the dower-house on the estate, and on one occasion at Mass in
the little Catholic church in the grounds I saw the ex-King
again. Throughout Mass I noticed him eyeing me keenly, and
I wondered whether the royal memory had placed me as the
only man in that group at the Hôtel Meurice who had failed to
kiss his hand in loyal homage.

During the Second World War my duties as a King's Messenger took me frequently to France. In 1940 I was in the New
York Bar in Paris discussing the war with a stranger. At that
time there were few of us who did not realise that Paris had
in fact already fallen and that it was full of French *embusqués,* fifth-
columnists and German officers in plain clothes, with their
uniforms hanging up in a hundred hotel-cupboards. It seemed
to me that the man I was talking to knew a little too much
not to be someone who knew a great deal more. I immediately

signalled to Harry behind the bar and whispered to him that at all costs he must keep the man talking while I telephoned the Deuxième Bureau. They agreed to send someone round at once, but the man must have realised that his vanity, the spy's Achilles heel, had betrayed him; when I returned to the bar he had fled. Harry had been unable to detain him. Ten days later Paris fell officially, just as the stranger at the bar had predicted in such detail. France was on her knees; Germany was at her throat.

I have always been fortunate in having many charming friends in Paris. Time can pass quickly in pleasant company but moves, I suppose, no more quickly than it did in the past. It is we who move the quicker and so often overtake it, particularly when we fly east by jet.

I remember the barman at the Hotel Gloria in Rio remarking in 1941 that I had not been in for a few days. I had, as it happened, in that short time flown south to Buenos Aires, over the Andes to Santiago, then north to Washington and back to Rio.

I was continually flying on this route as a King's Messenger with my 'crossed' bags; but this man, seeing me so often, assumed that I lived in Rio. In fact, it was only when I was staying overnight there that he saw me.

Father was afraid that I had inherited my restlessness from a great-uncle who spent his entire life travelling and whose greatest joy was to make a successful railway connection by only a split-second. For him, to travel was truly more satisfying than to arrive. We met uncle Edgar once on the old *Warwickshire* of the Bibby Line. He was in the smoke-room, seated well back in his chair and in the process or removing his shoes, which he did whenever he sat down.

Father, in his Old Wykehamist way, regarded this behaviour as eccentric, yet to this day I never travel by train or plane without taking off my shoes and donning bedroom-slippers. Once, at Georgetown in British Guiana, I left the plane while it was refuelling; the tropical heat had melted a part of the tarmac, and my slippers immediately sank into it. Suddenly, I found myself striding forward in stockinged feet.

I have stressed the fact that Uncle Edgar had been sitting well back in his chair when we met him: he suffered from kathedraphobia, which (I understand) is the name given to a dread of sitting too close to the edge of a chair and consequently falling off. I was spared the inheritance of this particular phobia, but like Uncle Edgar I am addicted to the sending of messages addressed to 'whomsoever', sealed in bottles and thrown into the ocean, whenever the opportunity presents itself. I believe that eccentric people live longer than the more normal. Uncle Edgar died in his ninetieth year, of old age it was rumoured.

Father, too, had idiosyncrasies. Though he was an extravagant man himself, when he was not otherwise occupied in the evening he used to enjoy going round the house, turning out lights in all unoccupied rooms. Father had four graves prepared for him: one in Anglesey, one in London, one in Berkhamstead and another in San Remo. In each of these places he had a house. 'Bury me in the nearest,' he said.

He also had a horror of strangers trespassing on the estate, and when he detected a place from which he might be overlooked, even from a long distance, he would immediately build a wall. He was jealous of his privacy, considering it one of the most important things that money could buy.

I have always been inquisitive about people when their appearance interests me or when I cannot place them. Once this led to a friend being summoned before the committee of his club. I was in the Conservative Club, drinking rather heavily with Dale Bourn, that delightful natural golfer, who won the French Amateur Championship; and I noticed a man sitting alone, of so severe a countenance that he looked like the undertaker destined to bury all other undertakers.

'Ask him who he is,' I said. 'It is absolutely necessary that we should know.' Dale swayed over to him.

'Young man,' I heard the man say in an icy Scottish accent, 'I'm a Writer to the Signet.'

'To the what?'

'To the Signet,' the angry man repeated. A hush followed,

broken by Dale's voice asking blandly: 'And does the bird ever answer?'

Father was continually making long-distance telephone calls, and when he did so he could usually be heard in any part of the house and in certain parts of the garden as well. He strongly believed, as people tend to who have lived before the telephone was universal, that the longer the distance the louder he had to shout.

He also believed that to speak to a foreigner and make him understand it was necessary to use broken English. I, myself, have always acted on the principle that in a foreign language it is better to be able to talk fluently rather than a little beautifully. Mother, whose accent in French was never perfect, was absolutely fluent; at dinner-parties where French was the common language, she completely outshone the gentlemen of the Foreign Office with their exquisitely enunciated but stilted phraseology.

In spite of the old adage[1] I regard French as an all-purpose language in which it should be simple either to clarify or dissemble, to make love or express loathing. One lovely day I was with an enchanting American girl driving in a *fiacre* in the Bois de Boulogne. Suddenly, as if to record his joy at being alive on such a spring morning, the horse entertained us to a *feu de joie*. Our old *cocher* raised his top-hat, leaned forward on his box the better to echo his horse's jubilation in this universal language, then, turning to us with a broad wink, remarked: 'Quelle belle musique '

I had been in love with this temperamental girl for at least a month. She spent hours in the pursuit of culture when all I wanted to do was drive in the Bois or idle on the *terrasse* of the Dôme or the Select. To enrich her mind she was studying the French classics from Molière and Racine to Balzac, Flaubert, Victor Hugo and even Proust, but of these famous dramatists and writers I knew it was the great Honoré who pleased her most, for one day she had remarked, 'The greatest, and I mean

[1] 'Speak Spanish to God, Italian to women, French to men and German to horses.'

E

the greatest, is Balls-ache.' On another occasion she was
rhapsodising over the Impressionists Manet, Degas and Renoir.
I had to be careful what I said, because she sometimes had the
idea that I was laughing at her when I was merely enjoying and
admiring her. On this particular occasion I unfortunately
mentioned Monet. Suddenly she turned on me, her blue eyes
blazing. 'You worship the golden calf! Napoloean was right
when he called you a nation of shopkeepers, you can think of
nothing but money!' She was very beautiful when she was
angry, and when I felt brave enough I enjoyed arousing her wrath.

Apart from being lusciously attractive, she had her own idea
of what was funny, and I noticed on an application form she was
filling up in detail for a French driving licence opposite *née* she
had written *retroussé*.

To a romantic in Paris the trees in the Bois are always in
leaf; in the Parc Monceau the old people are always taking their
ease in the shade under the foliage, and the white tables and
the bright sunshades of Pré Catelan and Armenoville are
for ever calling me. I have laughed and wept a little in Paris;
and until a man has loved and suffered in Paris, he has never
really lived. This is ridiculous of course, but it is a romantic's
view. Stendhal, perhaps the greatest of modern French writers,
was convinced that 'the women of Lancashire are so passionate
that they kill themselves for love'. He should have lived here-
after – to see 'Coronation Street'. And I have read about a
Frenchman who served with the R.A.F. after the fall of France
being overcome with emotion and nostalgia at the word
'Uddersfield, that dream-city where once he was stationed.
Yet the French are probably the most practical and unemotional
of peoples. Reprimanding me for becoming too friendly with
her daughter, a French mother said to me 'Une fois, oui. Deux
fois, oui. Mais trois fois, monsieur, c'est l'habitude.'

On my first visit to Paris after demobilisation, I was given a
letter of introduction to Madame Floris, who lived in the
Rue Caumartin. I took my letter along one afternoon with a card
on which I had written my address. At the apartment, a woman,
whom I later knew as Jeanette, answered the bell. In my politest

French I explained that I would be in Paris for at least three months, but it was my first duty and pleasure to present this letter of introduction and my respects to Madame Floris. I was a little surprised to be told that she received visitors only in the evening.

I was dining that night with an old French couple in Passy and I told them about the strange reception I had received at the Rue Caumartin. Later the old man drew me aside, and, out of the hearing of his wife, explained that it was not customary in Paris for the better type of brothels to open before five o'clock. It was at this moment of truth that I felt most deeply that Uncle Maurice, who had given me the letter of introduction, should have been more frank with me.

A few days later I had the pleasure of meeting Madame Floris, a somewhat severe but at the same time charming middle-aged woman who, as I later came to learn, was respected by her clientele and adored by her girls. They were of many nationalities: European, South American and Oriental. It was a house-of-all-nations. Thanks to my letter of introduction they had immediately accepted and treated me as a guest of Madame rather than a client.

Sometimes I would sit with the staff in the salon after the last visitor had left. The room would still be hung with tobacco smoke, and each girl in turn would call on Madame to check her earnings. The empty champagne-bottles were counted, the glasses washed, the ash-trays emptied.

Jeanette, who used to answer the door and call warningly in her Breton French, 'On monte', might be drinking anisette with Marie, who was in charge of the bed linen and hand-towels. The girls were in their dressing-gowns; the night's work was over and peace had fallen on the house. For economy the brilliant chandeliers were dimmed, and there was a crisp rustle of notes and a clink of coins as the girls counted their *petits cadeaux*. It may well have been then that I first realised the brutality and tenderness of money.

The girls seldom quarrelled, but when they did it was invariably a physical quarrel, fierce and short and usually concerned with their pimps – who, in most cases, represented the only private life they had. Madame Floris, rather unkindly, refused to allow them into the house.

The girls' lives were dedicated to a common purpose, so that instinctively – as in a naval ward-room – controversial subjects were avoided. I was accepted in a brotherly, slightly incestuous way, for it was soon understood that I listened so intensely to all they had to say only because I was anxious to improve my knowledge of the language.

Much of their conversation was earnest, even when charged with mockery, and sometimes revealed to me, quite unexpectedly, an undercurrent of sexual tenderness and compassion. In the half-light, some of them would sit contentedly as if recalling the pleasant moments of the evening; others, it seemed, were dreaming back into another and secret life. Most were silent, as if for everything that was said there was something more important that must remain unsaid.

In this atmosphere of quiet there was perceptible the stealthy animal smell of tired young bodies. I, too, rested in what I liked to imagine romantically, was the company of *jeunes filles en fleur,* for I had just been reading the first volume of Proust's masterpiece, then unknown in England; nor did I realise then that his young girls were in fact his young boys.

I never heard a surname spoken in that house. It was always *Mademoiselle* Celeste, *Mademoiselle* Josie, Chiquita, Olga, Suzette, yet each one must have possessed a surname recorded somewhere in the book of life.

After this, when anyone was kind enough to give me a letter of introduction I always hoped it would take me into a world as amusing and sad and even masked as Madame Floris's salon and her house of mirrored ceilings.

Around that time there was a story being told about my boyhood friend Duncan Laird, whose father was chairman of Cammell Laird's. He had announced at his club that he was going to the West Indies. A friend suggested he might like to have a letter of introduction to the Governor of one of the islands. In due course, on his arrival there, Duncan presented his introduction and was invited to a garden party at Government House. This was followed by an invitation to dinner. When the Governor's lady had left the room and the port-decanter was on the table, the Governor expressed his pleasure at his guest's presence, but confessed, to Duncan's embarrassment, that the man who had written the letter of introduction was completely unknown to him.

When Duncan returned to London he encountered the man at the club. 'You're an awful shit,' Duncan informed him. 'You gave me a letter of introduction to someone you don't even know.'

'My dear fellow,' the man replied, 'you don't seriously think that I would give you a letter of introduction to anyone I did know?' Duncan, the kindest of men, was so amused that he forgot to give the fellow the kick in the backside he had promised himself the pleasure of donating.

I had, at an early age, learned the usefulness of being on good terms with barmen. The good barman combines in himself many qualities a bank manager could never aspire to. Eric, the delightful barman for so many years at the casinos in Cannes and Deauville, once told me: 'I don't get to bed until five in the morning. I have to remember how to mix a hundred cocktails. I have to answer questions without informing and enquire without questioning. I have to know when to give credit and when not. I have to break an egg without breaking the yolk and smile when I've got a hangover, In fact, I'm like a whore; I've to be everything to every man and it's a miracle I'm still happily married.'

Harry's New York Bar in Paris in the early twenties was a rendezvous for foreign correspondents and expatriate Americans. I used to look in there frequently in spite of the stench of Harry's black cigars.

One evening I saw Scott Fitzgerald's pale face peering at me through the reek. He had been there for some time, obviously upholding his reputation as a drinker of high calibre. Harry, at that time, was compiling a book listing cocktails and their ingredients, and long drinks too. He was running short of recipes. Scott and I decided it was up to us to invent a new one for him, so with his full co-operation we went to work.

For this type of exploratory and creative work Scott Fitz-gerald was an ideal and industrious colleague. With every drink under the sun and moon to hand, the concoction of mixtures can be interesting and even confusing. To help us remember what we had already mixed and tasted, Scott started making notes.

Unfortunately, no sooner had we mixed a drink and sampled it than we forgot the taste of the one before. So Scott suggested that we should sip rather than drink.

We proceeded on these lines for a short time, then started lining them up on the bar so that we could check and recheck them. This we did conscientiously, interrupted only for our *petit besoin* as our French nannies called it. But soon we gave up writing down the recipes because by that time his notes had become too difficult to decipher. As dawn broke over Paris we agreed that we had at long last evolved the perfect formula.

'Let's now mix it in a large shaker,' Scott suggested, 'for, our work done, we can now enjoy the fruits of our labour. Now is the time to celebrate.'

I cannot remember what the drink comprised. It contained something of everything and tasted strong. Held up to the light, it blazed a warning in rainbow colours, and the first swallow was like the breath of a Bunsen burner sparked off with a dash of dynamite. We drank like men determined to drown the taste and, with the help of those others in the bar and to a great lifting of glasses, we christened it 'Desert Healer'.

Later I watched with a sense of detachment as Scott tacked his way to the telephone-booth. A few weeks later, it seemed to me, I saw him returning. He was sailing into a head-wind, tacking to port, then gybing, until he almost came about, before finally coming alongside.

Though he was leaning close and speaking confidentially, it was as though he were speaking from a great distance. Faintly I could hear his husky voice explaining: 'I'm glad I telephoned, because it's not whisky that Zelda wants, its rum and vodka; but she doesn't want it after all, because she still has some left in the bottle from last night, when I was supposed to have taken back vodka and gin, and I took back a bottle of Scotch.'

By this time I had lost all coherence and it was as if I had put on a stranger's reading glasses, for Scott, my charming unspeakable friend, seemed to advance and recede as in a dance with solemn, measured tread. Eventually a taxi was called to take us home. I had only to cross the narrow street to the Daunou, which Scott didn't know, so he was mystified when I stepped in at one door of the taxi and immediately out of the other.

We met again two months later in Cannes at Duncan Orr-Lewis's Villa Valetta, which he then occupied. Strange to relate, he had an advance copy of Harry's book and in it, boldly listed for all to read, with a full acknowledgement, was our precious 'Desert Healer'.

Duncan Orr-Lewis, with the latest of his lovely wives, had been a dear friend of mine from the time we were boys. On one occasion at Villa Zero, which he had then made his home, at a large cocktail party, I heard a woman's voice behind me say: 'My dear Duncan, you should know by now that I loathe Dubonnet.' Then came Duncan's soft voice: 'Madam, I am not asking you to drink a Dubonnet, I am merely asking you to meet Monsieur Dubonnet!'

At that time I probably believed anything any woman told me, as long as it was something I wished to hear. I spoilt them in small ways. If I was dining with a girl, I would bribe the woman in the ladies' cloakroom not to accept a tip. I would have the table-waiter wear a huge carnation. The orchestra would play her favourite tunes and the chef would bring the dishes to the table, with each course on the menu named after her. The head-waiter served the *omelette surprise* and the *sommelier* did a minuet around the table with the champagne, the coffee, the liqueurs and the special Abdulla rose-tipped cigarettes.

By the time we left the table she was prepared to believe that I had created the world. Before I took her home we would visit Les Halles, the great Paris market, for that was the moment when the fruit and the flowers were flowing in from the countryside.

I was always fond of *crêpes suzette*. The pancakes were served in a sauce of melted sugar and orange-juice mixed with butter; at the last moment M. Joseph, the proprietor of the Marivaux, with a flash of genius, poured on a glass of Armagnac so that a blue flame would light up the dish and attract the attention of the audience.

While I was on a visit to London an important event happened in my life. Gertrude Lawrence, who was appearing at the Vaudeville Theatre in a Charlot revue, introduced me to her cousin Victoria Banks, who had taken the stage name of Ruby Lorraine. Ruby was much in the news at the time as the model for Raphael Kirschner's pin-ups, world famous and much prized. Her face was as lovely and tender as an Eastern dawn, and she had an irresistible personality. And I knew that she was not indifferent to me, for I had pursued my courtship with ardour and some skill. To avoid family interference we met in secret and arranged a trysting-place beneath a rather drab little tree in Kensington Gardens near our home in Lancaster Gate.

Here I determined to ask her to marry me, and at a suitable time before our meeting I sent out a footman into the gardens with a large basket of crimson roses and a reel of silver wire. As instructed, he attached the blooms to the branches, where they blazed, bright and odorous, mute symbols of my passion. That afternoon I was accepted, but our engagement remained – as the proposal had been made – *sub rosa*.

Two months later we were married, against the advice of my parents and those friends who had forgotten how foolish it is to be young. We spent our honeymoon in Paris, Deauville, Biarritz and San Sebastián. It is difficult, looking back, to remember when the honeymoon in terms of travelling ended, probably in the apartment which I had taken at 5 Rue des Eaux in the XVIme. I have always found Paris to be a city where it is possible to live as many lives as one's constitution permits. We were both bohemians at heart, and we were as happy and at home in the Dôme, the Rotonde, the Dingo and the Closerie des Lilas as we were in the Ritz, the Meurice or the Lancaster.

Friends would arrive from England and America who wanted to visit the Russian *émigré* cabarets of Montmartre or the café-bistros and dance-halls of the Quartier Latin, so it would have been difficult to settle down to domestic existence even had we wished.

There was the glorious racing on Sundays at Longchamp and Auteuil; and visits to the charming restaurants of the Bois. It was the Paris of Sem, who caricatured so brilliantly the café-restaurant life of that period.

André Letellier, the owner of *Le Journal*, with his current mistress and her exquisite jewellery, became a close friend. He was many years older, but introduced us into his own fabulous world of pleasure. We became habitués of Ciro's, the Café de Paris, Voisin, Zelli's Royal Box and Le Jardin de ma Sœur. We had entered that 'international world' *interdit au gens serieux*.

Our financial position during this 'keep the change' period was sometimes strained, but we were able to return hospitality at Claridge on the Champs-Elysées, the newest hotel in Paris, of which Father was a director and principal shareholder.

One day I heard that Gertie Lawrence was in a nursing home in the Rue Spontini, off the Avenue Bois de Boulogne, so I went to see her. It was, fortunately, nothing serious; in fact she was probably feeling better than I was, for I had been at Maxim's until the early hours of the morning. I brought her white lilac with the inevitable bunch of grapes. She was witty and amusing as always, and I left only when two other visitors arrived. A surprise awaited me, however, in the street below, for as I hailed a taxi to the kerb, outside the nursing home, my beautiful lilac was flung from the window and landed squarely on my fevered head. The simple explanation that Gertie gave me later was that she had always looked on white lilac as unlucky. This was not wholly true; the fact was that Gertie, unlike most women, disliked flowers that weren't growing, and in fact never wore them.

As soon as she was completely recovered she dined with us.

Some days later as we were driving to a *soirée de gala* she insisted on stopping the cab outside a theatre in Montmartre, explaining that she had always wanted to see and hear the performance of a man who styled himself 'Le grand Pétomane,' and she

E2

had reason to believe that he was appearing there. Gertie was
to suffer a disappointment for when I went in to enquire I was
informed that, alas, that 'The great wind-expulsion expert is on
holiday.' Thus these two great artists were destined never to
meet.

That Easter we were at Le Touquet, and I sent my father an
Easter egg. It was cream matt-surfaced with the fleur-de-lis
design repeated in *marée blue* and the egg was encircled with a
satin ribbon in a paler shade, tied in a handsome bow. It had
to be rather a large egg because in it I had stuffed all my out-
standing bills. The view held generally by the family was that
my little joke was in the worst possible taste, particularly as they
were at the receiving end of the gift, but none of them understood Father as I did. As usual, in his generous way, he paid up.
It was, I regret to say, not the last of many thousands.

Looking back I wonder whether the years spent in the army
– sustained by the Government at whatever cost, and living
quite literally from moment to moment – had not made this
seem to many of us a permanent condition of life. It was
estimated that it took ten men to keep one soldier in the line,
which meant that the Government had spent thousands on each
of us, despite our meagre pay. This may be a far-fetched idea; but
at that time the world certainly seemed full of young men with
money to burn and friends to dance with round the bonfire.

My only concern was the flow of letters I was receiving from
Father urging me to return to London. He wanted me to choose
a career. If it became necessary he would finance me. I promised
him I would think his generous offer over.

I hated the idea of having to leave Paris with its delicious
atmosphere, the delectable smells that wafted through its
streets and gardens, the roasting chestnuts of the winter months,
the lilac and garlic, the burned-up petrol of summer; and over
all, in season and out, the pungent reek of Algerian tobacco.
In London I might still drink the finest wines, but I would
miss my chocolate and *brioche* for breakfast.

But there was no way out. Father had to be placated, and
that meant going into business.

10

A False Start

I HAD already met several business tycoons, denizens of the overworld, in Paris and London and I had not been impressed. They had one thing in common, a certain ill-masked ruthlessness. They were even capable of ordering flowers *by telephone*! Invariably the tycoon tries to persuade himself that he has the power to control other lives and even events. He knows the value of everything except what money will not buy. Even his women become discouraged when they realise that he has more money than they can spend.

His only hope of saving his soul is to be a patron of the arts, naturally without expecting artists to sit too often at his table. If he wants a title he can subscribe to party funds; but this is tricky because at the same time the right charities must also be donated to. He has usually accumulated compulsive riches that he has not the taste or intelligence to spend with enjoyment. A man can wear only one suit at a time, however often he changes during the day. He suspects that without his money he would have no friends, indeed, he is uncertain if he has any with it. He learns to distrust even those foolish enough to trust him. The happiest thing that can be said about him is that he can be in only one place at a time.

I remember one fabulously wealthy man, no doubt envied by many, who invited himself to a birthday party given by a friend of mine. It was only a small gathering, and from the moment he arrived his cold, calculating presence killed the party stone-dead.

Even if I had possessed the brains and industry to make a

commercial career I would rather have chosen to go in for
some sort of creative work. I wanted dearly to be a writer. But
what had I to write about? I had no eggs for the omelette.
Now that Father's patience was clearly coming to an end
I wrote telling him that I would like to join Eveleigh Nash in
his publishing house, a suggestion that had already been mooted.

In spite of the tireless enthusiasm I had brought to living
an aimless life and the earnestness with which I had applied
myself to the pursuit of pleasure, books and reading of every
description had always been my first love. If I had to work
I was determined that it must be enjoyable work. So Father
invested £8000 with Eveleigh Nash, and I joined as a director
with a salary of £1000 a year.

My work naturally threw me into the company of every
type of writer, from William Le Queux to Cunninghame
Graham and Robert Hichens, from John Collier to Edgar Lee
Masters and Wyndham Lewis. Eveleigh Nash, who had recently
sold *Nash's Magazine* to Hearst, was a remarkably well read and
astute Scotsman. He had realised the great future of publishing
cheap reprints of great or famous books. We brought out a
half-crown series called Nash's Great Novel Library. The
cheap rights were acquired from the other publishers before
they realised what our intention was, so that it might be said
that in some cases we had the best authors on almost every
other publisher's list.

Our first list contained works by Hardy, Conrad, Stevenson,
A. E. W. Mason, Jeffrey Farnol, de Vere Stacpoole and Hichens.
The Great Novel Library and the Famous Fiction Library were
equally successful: it was Father's investment that made this
possible. About this time Evan Morgan, Lord Tredegar,
invited me to a Catholic convocation at Birmingham. We spent
a wonderfully amusing and instructive week with Belloc and
Chesterton, whose conversation suggested two brilliant duel-
lists engaged in friendly combat. We wrote several articles for
Catholic papers which were duly translated and published in
the Italian Press.

Three months later I received a letter and scroll attached to a certificate, sealed and stamped by the Vatican, appointing me a Knight of the Holy Sepulchre, which, I am told, gave me the right to legitimise bastards.

My father had built Ruby and me a house in Ennismore Street, one of the first non-basement houses in Knightsbridge, strategically situated between a well-stocked public house on the corner of the mews and a French convent on the opposite side of the street.

My wife chose grey sycamore furniture inlaid with ivory for her bedroom; but in the drawing-room we had a rosewood piano inlaid with a floral design, pink and green and white. Painted furniture and buhl pieces set off with brocaded runners in purple and green, gold-braided like altar-cloths. In the dining-room the white and gold table with its oval mahogany top with chairs in similar design, each one with arms, had been shipped from Paris together with the marble chimney-pieces.

To reassemble the fireplaces I had to employ Italians from Clerkenwell. They spent a large part of the day teaching us to sing bawdy Neapolitan songs in the kitchen, eating macaroni and drinking Chianti, which we bought from Luigi's in Soho.

Except in the bedrooms, which were lined in pink *toile de Jouy* linen, the house had glass doors and the floors were parquet, for Father had given us many of the exquisite Persian rugs of which he was a collector. They were deep red Tekke Turcomans, mahogany-shaded Baluchistans, saddle-bags, prayer-rugs and a beautiful, gay, golden and glowing crimson Agra that must have taken the prisoners in the jail a lifetime to weave.

In my bedroom I had a Khiva, which, in damp weather, came to life under my bare feet with the smell of the goats from whose hair it had been woven. Some of the rugs with their wordless language I still possess, but the little silk prayer-rug made for a princess to kneel on disappeared like so many things and people I have loved. Father had bought the chandeliers and many of the wall-lights in Venice and had them shipped to London.

In the drawing-room Charles Buchel had painted a perfect

trompe-l'œil, almost too deceiving. It represented an open french window leading onto a green lawn with a distant view of bright flowering beds. One could almost hear the sounds of a garden and smell the flowers.

One day, seeing a new, short-sighted manservant crossing the room towards this painting with a tray of decanters and glasses, I asked him where he was going; and he replied that on such a beautiful day he thought we might like our drinks served in the garden.

In the winter my wife, in spite of central heating, insisted on having the fires banked up like the engines of the Great Western Railway, so that the chimneys caught fire approximately once a month.

When this happened, our little friends the French nuns would come running into their garden, where they would stand grouped like a choir, pointing upwards with their white hands, chanting in unison, 'De chimberlays . . . de chimberlays . . .' This delightful performance, like an expert from Puccini's *Suor Angelica,* would continue until the fire-engine arrived to drown their voices with its discordant banging, bashing and bustle.

The men who leapt from every part of the panting monster would then invade the house, dragging python coils of rubber tubing tapering to brilliantly polished brass nozzles. It took long hours to clear up the mess they made and wash the empty glasses they left behind, for firemen, I soon discovered, were, like journalists and wind-instrumentalists, thirsty men.

We still spent as much time abroad as my duties as a publisher would allow: a week at Monte Carlo in the winter, a fortnight at Deauville in August, and the first week of September in Biarritz.

I was now able to see more of my family than when we had lived in Paris. My brother Denys had taken a lease of the St James's Theatre. In addition to this he was studying orchestration under Frank Bridge and was composing music played regularly by the B.B.C., especially his 'Nocturne' and 'In Linden Time'. We had many interests in common, so we had many disagreements. He had a nice sense of humour, both sweet and sour; on one occasion I cabled him from America – 'Do you know Uncle Charles's address in New York?' and his reply came back 'Yes'.

Brian had come down from Cambridge, 'with colours flying,' in time to save Lloyd George's sister-in-law from drowning, for which he was awarded the Royal Humane Society's Medal; and he had married Sofia Buchanan, a lovely dark-eyed daughter of the Counsellor at the Chilean Embassy.

Tristram had joined the Irish Guards and picked an Irish flower, Barbara Finucane, out of that garden of flowers for his wife. In the regiment, in due course, he rose to the rank of colonel. He was appointed and continually reappointed deputy provost-marshal because of his charm and tact.

It was on one of King George VI's birthdays many years later that he was in attendance at the Trooping when he overheard a delightful example of the monarch's caustic Windsor-Mountbatten manner when he was displeased. The Officer Commanding the London District said to the king, 'We have decided, as the drill takes up so much time, to dispense with guardsmen carrying canes; that is, sir, subject to your permission.'

'Certainly, do away–way with th–th–the cane.' the monarch stammered in reply. 'The–en the men will be able to – walk about with bo–oth their hands in–n their pockets.' But the king could laugh at himself.

My friend Pat Murphy, of Crookhaven in West Cork, was one day walking with the Dean of Windsor in the grounds when they met the head gardener with his dog at his heels. At this moment George VI appeared on the scene and looked at at the dog with some surprise; for it is, as everyone knows, a strict rule that no dog is allowed in a Royal Park without a lead, however much they may roam and frisk in the public pleasaunces. The gardener was greatly dismayed.

'I hoped your majesty would not object. The dog is almost human,' said the gardener in apology.

'In th–th–that case,' stuttered the king, 'I suppose that m–m–makes two of us who c–c–can nearly t–t–talk.'

My sister Ailsa had married Dick Rawlinson, whose first novel, *Sheep's Clothing,* we published. This was the beginning of his career as successful playwright and film writer. Monica had married Eddie FitzClarence, Lord Munster's heir, who was still serving in the Irish Guards. His father had commanded the regiment and had been awarded a Victoria Cross in the South African War; he was killed in the first European war. The twins were still at Downside, and my young sisters used to be driven daily to the Convent of the Sacred Heart in Holyhead, where they went to school.

One afternoon Father, seeing the car about to leave to collect them, instructed the young chauffeur, who had only recently joined the staff, to bring back his Three Nuns. On his return an hour later the chauffeur reported to Father that the Reverend Mother had said that her nuns were strictly forbidden to leave the Convent. (Three Nuns is the well-known brand of pipe-tobacco that used to advise smokers that 'properly to enjoy Three Nuns, do not rub or tease, but press down firmly'.)

Nancy had married my dear friend Louis Drexel and I had been his best man at St Margaret's, doing the usual ridiculous thing which made me famous among my friends. I gave the ring to the head bell-ringer and put his ten-guinea fee in my pocket. Fortunately he called my attention to this. Nancy's marriage and Ailsa's both produced great lawyers – Victor Drexel, today a leading attorney in America, and Sir Peter Rawlinson, the Queen's Counsel and Privy Councillor in England.

We used to make occasional visits to Anglesey where most of the family spent the entire summer, either at Ravenspoint itself or in one of the cottages on the estate. Life there was a constant source of amusement. Each member of the family had a friend staying, and there was a constant ebb and flow of welcome guests.

Fives, golf and cricket matches were always being arranged; and a play performed in Holyhead and produced by Denys and Robert Loraine had become an annual event. Some of us, rather reluctantly, took parts, and the funds went to charity.

Father spent more time abroad, but somehow he was always there when anything important had to be decided. In many ways he lived his own life among us. When he took a walk, it was alone; when he went to church, he worshipped – alone – that English Protestant God who had the right ideas about the British Empire, cricket and banking. He would undoubtedly sooner have seen the last priest than the last king.

At home Mother, with her dynamic personality, was the central figure around whom everything revolved. In her delightfully unconventional way she was miraculously both hostess and guest at the same time. O'Rourke, a Dublin character first and butler as an after-thought, together with our wonderful cook Mrs Eves ran the house and the domestic staff, though they were always subject to Mother's interference when she felt like it.

Mother had come of an Irish family long resident in Chile. She had been born in Valparaiso and was suckled, as the custom was, by an Indian woman. Her father had made his fortune in nitrates by the time he was forty-five and had retired to live in England, bringing Mother, who was then sixteen, with him. I remember her telling me that she had arrived in London with so many chinchilla coats and wraps and skins that she used to give them to the servants to trim their dresses. The next two years she spent at Madame Lalonde's finishing school in Paris, and the following year she married my father after a whirlwind courtship. Her background had never been an ordinary one, nor was it to become one, for we lived in an age when a certain careless, carefree way of life was known only to the comparative few; and this was a way of life to which Mother brought her genius for the unconventional.

She had no money sense, and she would feel she was economising if she took a bus to Harrods, even if she spent £300 when she got there. Father was probably to blame for this, because from the time when they were first married he paid all her bills, and it was only later in life that she had her own bank account. She believed that as long as there was a cheque left in her book there must be money for her in the bank.

She was a great conversationalist and raconteuse, with a

dazzling gift for exaggeration, like most of the Irish. Though she had no suspicion of a brogue, her words, clear-cut and cadenced, captivated her listeners. Mother had a lovely way of coining her own words; at the Irish Linen Shop in Bond Street she was heard to say to the assistant, 'I want the handkerchiefs henpecked', and on a more serious occasion when a man had been arrested in Holyhead for raping a girl, she remarked grimly, 'He ought to be castinated.'

She disliked people *en masse*, whoever they were, whatever their origin; and I'm afraid she had little sense of reality. She once remarked to Pat Kirwan: 'They've raised the tax on manservants from seven-and-sixpence to a guinea. No wonder there's unemployment in the country.'

During the Second World War I was serving at the Admiralty when the name of Nicholas Monsarrat cropped up. I believe it was to do with those short-listed for the next destroyer commands. Monsarrat had distinguished himself in frigates, and it was a rare honour for a R.N.V.R. officer even to be considered for destroyers. At once my mind went back to Ravenspoint and the two small Monsarrat boys who were friends of the twins. Nicholas, who later wrote that superb book *The Cruel Sea*, writes of Ravenspoint in his autobiography *Life is a Four-Letter Word*.

Foremost among these were our new next-door neighbours, the Graysons, who had arrived soon after the war. Sir Henry Grayson was a Liverpool ship-owning baronet of some consequence; he had substantial resources, unlimited charm, and a family of twelve children. They were a wholly fascinating family, with just that touch of fantasy appropriate to a fairy-tale world.

I forget the names of the elder children, but the last five, roughly our contemporaries, were three ravishing girls – Monica, Meryl, and Angela – and the Twins, Ambrose and Godfrey. The latter were the sort of Twins who demand the use of capital letters: they were inseparable, deeply loyal to each other, and so naughty that Denys[1] and I had the novel

---

[1] Nicholas's brother, not mine. R.G.

experience of being held up to them as good examples. This was quite enough to invest them with a special degree of significance.

The Graysons, having bought a substantial section of the coast adjoining Hafod, built and settled down in the largest house ever likely to adorn Trearddur Bay: a huge, rambling place, with courtyards, walled gardens, a squash-court, and sufficient garage-space and stabling to accommodate the cars and horses which fourteen people, their husbands, wives, families, and friends were bound to acquire.

They were almost a separate community themselves: as the elder children got married, houses and cottages were built for them nearby. Indeed, Hafod itself eventually became a sort of Naboth's Vineyard entirely surrounded by Grayson territory. We did not mind: hospitable, unexacting, and never dull, they were ideal neighbours to have.

Their house was called Ravenspoint. We often used to go over to play with the three girls or the Twins, climbing the stile in our own garden wall, crossing the next field which sometimes yielded a useful crop of mushrooms, and then making our way over the lawn to the house itself. It was like stepping on to a very crowded stage full of unrelated characters from different plays.

Some of them would greet us, particularly Lady Grayson herself, who had the welcoming charm and unfailing kindness which too often one looks for in vain outside the classier kind of novel; others had forgotten who we were, or had never known; others still, themselves visitors, took us for Grayson children and discovered a family likeness. Cars drove up, disgorging fresh arrivals who would often be quarrelling: we would be invited to play charades, to retrieve tennis-balls, to have a cup of a very special kind of chocolate which had just arrived from Zürich.

Once, from an aircraft which had crash-landed in a nearby field, a young man in evening dress stepped out and made his way to join us on the terrace. He received an uproarious greeting, being, I think, a cousin. Weaving a quick and graceful path among us as we sat there, small Italian footmen in yellow liveries darted to and fro, like goldfish doomed by fate to wait on their larger neighbours. Off the stage one sometimes heard them cursing, in torrential Italian, a delivery boy who could only answer in Welsh.

Somewhere on the outer rim of the circle, tall, dignified, benign, and very handsome, Sir Henry Grayson gave his flawless interpretation of the part of the head of the family. He was not the sort of man whom even twelve children, their relatives, and their friends, could ever surprise or dismay.

There were fourteen dogs.

When we had done our duty by the grown-ups, we went off to play with the younger children. The three girls were about Felicity's age, the Twins were contemporaries of Denys: I hovered uneasily between the two camps, varying an ambition I could not yet define with a condescension I was hardly entitled to. But girls being what they are, I usually ended up with the Twins. They had an Italian nurse called Providentia, a rather unstable character (as well she might be) who frequently burst into tears at some fresh enormity of the Twins, and whom they then comforted and charmed back to laughter again.

It is difficult to describe how odd these supernumerary players, the Italian footmen and the nurse Providentia, seemed to us, when they were first set against our staid Welsh back-cloth. But when we got used to them they grew, like the Graysons themselves, to be an essential part of Trearddur Bay, and one we would have missed tremendously.

To prevent the Twins quarrelling, their toys had either to be duplicated or specially designed to accommodate both of them at once. They had a huge toy motor-car built on these lines, in which they rode tandem at a break-neck speed: there was a two-seated, square-ended punt wherein, sitting facing each other, they would row wildly in opposite directions, using the most hair-raising language at the tops of their voices while the water churned to boiling foam and

Providentia, clasping her hands, screamed directions and threats from the bank.

Left to themselves, the Twins quarrelled and sometimes fought, but if an outsider ever took a hand they abandoned everything and, welded into a furious alliance, defied all comers.

We always enjoyed the time we spent over at Ravenspoint; there was an endless variety of things to do and to learn. This large and lively family, different from any we had known before, made our own nursery seem little more than a retreat for the shy and the timid; and until Denys and I took permanently to the water we thought it by far the best way of spending the day. But perhaps, even as we played there, the sea was beginning subtly to pull.

Ravenspoint, standing high up on the southerly arm of the bay, commanded a magnificent view of the whole coast-line nearly to South Stack lighthouse. On rough days the waves, surging in with the full force of the gale behind them, swept past in successive mile-long crests, piling up until they broke in a white flurry and fell thunderously on to the beach. One wanted to ride in with them, in some tough and gallant craft which refused to sink.

In one corner of the garden, on a jutting headland with a steep fall to the sea, a figure-head from an old sailing-ship had been set up. It represented a buxom goddess with black hair and gilded eye-lashes, who, turning her back on these strange mortals, stared across the moving water towards the Cardigan Hills. Staring with her, we sometimes suspected that she had the right idea.

The twins, who were only a few years younger than Nicholas, had the gift of getting away with anything they had already decided upon. One evening Father and Mother were going to a reception given by Lady Londonderry, who, with Mrs Ronnie Greville, was the leading political hostess of that period. Mother was looking lovely and Father was resplendent in his English, French, Italian and Belgian orders. At the last moment the twins, then aged about seven, decided to go with them in Mother's Daimler, for the ride.

When they arrived at Londonderry House the footman opened the car door and Mother and Father got out and entered the house. At the same moment Lord Birkenhead happened to be leaving and, seeing the car with the open door, he immediately stepped in and ensconced himself between the twins, who had by that time moved onto the back seat. He then ordered Cumberland, the chauffeur, to drive him to his house in Grosvenor Gardens. Smoking a long cigar and regaled with an elegant sufficiency of brandy, he appeared to be entirely unconscious of the small boy seated on either side of him. Arrived at Grosvenor Gardens he waved an airy farewell to Cumberland, mounted the steps to his home and was gone.

The twins, in their turn, were quite unconscious of the fact that the man who had been seated between them was the Lord Chancellor and the second personage of the realm.

Before long a new generation of nephews and lovely nieces were coming into flower. And when the twins had reached an age of something approaching discretion one could still be disconcerted by a niece. My little niece Jane's passion for flowers, for instance, resulted in my incorrect behaviour in the presence of Royals.

One day I was on my way to a Royal Garden Party when I decided to go into Kensington Gardens where my little niece and her nanny were spending the afternoon. Before I left them, Jane had picked me a huge bunch of daisies which she insisted on putting in my buttonhole. On the way to the palace I placed the daisies for safe-keeping in the lining of my top hat, because I knew that I would be seeing Jane again that evening, and that she would take no excuses for the absence of the buttonhole.

I had met the late Duke of Kent, then Prince George, on several week-ends when I was staying with the Howard de Waldens at Chirk Castle and at Humphrey and Poots Butler's home in London. At the party he hailed me over. I removed my hat and jerked my head down in formal court style, and a cascade of daisies fell on my shoulders.

'There's an explanation for everything; tell me about it later,' he said, laughing. He knew that we would probably meet that evening at the Butlers' home in Connaught Square.

There I explained why the daisies had fallen from my hat. He told me that he had once been staying at a country house and after dinner his host insisted on taking him to a barn, where he promised to show him an unusual sight. On their arrival, his host stationed him in a dark corner of the barn facing a large barrel filled with water. The entire surface was covered with floating corks. Behind it was a large bin of corn.

For some time they stood in silence broken only by the occasional hoot of an owl and the breathing of the night. Suddenly they heard a faint slithering and tapping sound. Prince George told the story well. I could see the two men waiting in the eerie darkness until the approaching shadow took on the shape of a glittering-eyed, well-fed rat. It was the first of a procession of rats, and each one leapt straight into the barrel, until it became a squealing cauldron of death.

To the Prince this apparently suicidal behaviour of the rats was inexplicable. His host, a cross between Leonardo da Vinci and Heath Robinson, explained that the rats had been getting at his corn. He noted that they always came from the same direction on their route across the barn. As soon as he had plotted the course they took he had placed across it an upturned barrel on which he nailed closely fitting corks. The rats thereafter became accustomed to using the barrel and the corks as a spring-board to reach the corn-bin, their final objective.

It was only on that particular night that he had turned the barrel over, filled it with water, and floated corks on the surface. As the Prince had said, there is always an explanation for everything and an answer to every question.

II

Vienna, Wagons-lits and the Mysterious Machine

IT was not long before I realised that publishing was not my *métier*. Eventually I resigned my position with the firm, and my younger brother Brian, who was reading for the Bar, agreed to take my place. He was capable and hard-working, with a personality which endeared him to everyone he met, so that I suspect Eveleigh Nash was only too delighted at the new arrangement.

Meanwhile I made one or two other abortive ventures into business. One of these arose out of a visit to Vienna. I had always had a great longing to see that city. The old Emperor Franz Joseph was dead and the grand dukes had retired to the Riviera; but most of the Viennese had known them and grown up with them and suffered them, for they were certainly an unruly lot. Otto, riding on his great black charger down the Kärtnering, met a funeral cortège. He immediately ordered the four pall-bearers to remove the coffin from the hearse and hold it aloft. He then proceeded to leap over it, after which the cortège was allowed to proceed. A delightful story for the person in the coffin to tell on his arrival at his destination. On another occasion he shocked the American Ambassador and his lady when he descended from a private room at Sacher's Hotel stark naked except for his belt and sword.

I travelled to Vienna on the Orient Express. In comparison with American trains it was vastly overrated. Its chief interest was the number of countries through which it ran on its route to

Istanbul. I met a blue-eyed blonde on the train, the type who, had she been English, would have used the expression 'ever so'. I invited her to dinner, and as the wine flowed freely she told me the story of part of her life.

She was the only daughter in a poor *rentier* family living just outside Brussels. She was a girl of courage and had no fear of a fate worse than death, so by the time she was seventeen she had learned to find her way about the city to such good purpose that she decided on a change: instead of her occasional visits to the capital from her home, she would, in future, make occasional visits to her home from the capital. She had decided also that the quickest way to a man's portfolio was to persuade him to open it in his hotel bedroom.

She frequented the Palace Hotel, where she met middle-aged and elderly businessmen with an occasional diplomat thrown in. In the meantime she had rented an apartment to which she admitted no one. Every Sunday she visited her home, taking with her a hamper of food and two bottles of champagne. For a girl so young that was a thoughtful thing to do, and it was appreciated by her parents.

With her steadily mounting balance at the bank it looked as if she would continue indefinitely the life she had found both interesting, for she was socially inclined, and profitable, because she had no intention of remaining poor. Then she told me how good fortune had caused her to meet Gustave, and how Gustave at once fell desperately in love with her.

This meeting took place at the Palace Hotel, for he was on the friendliest terms with the porters there. Gustave, she explained was connected with a highly important business group involved in great international affairs, but all that interested her at the time was that she loved Gustave and Gustave loved her. Indeed, he showed so much concern about her future that, instructed by him, she found herself once a fortnight standing in the foyer of the hotel in her little grey coat and skirt. A short time later her pigskin suitcase and travelling-rug would be brought down from her room, a room she never occupied.

In her handbag there was always a return ticket to Budapest, lipstick, rouge and the latest novel by Colette. Invariably there would be a man, the unconscious victim, usually middle-aged or elderly, who would also be waiting for a taxi to catch the same train. What more natural than that they should share the taxi; for it seemed transport was always difficult to procure.

Sharing the taxi usually led to sharing a *wagon-lit* on the train, for by some unfortunate misunderstanding, there had always been a mistake over mademoiselle's reservation, and the only unoccupied berth was in this gentleman's *wagon-lit*.

The whole set-up functioned so smoothly that Yvonne became a regular traveller on the Orient Express. She had even learned to accommodate her thoughts and movements to the short-long-long-short beat of the wheels and the less regular swinging of the bogies.

Mission accomplished, she would return to Brussels and produce whatever *cadeaux* she had been given on the train. Anything she earned Gustave would scrupulously bank for her in their joint account. He would naturally deduct money for the rent of the apartment into which he had now himself thoughtfully moved, at the same time allocating a fixed sum for her dress allowance, cigarettes, cosmetics, drinks in bars, etc. As she explained, 'It was like having my own secretary,' adding, with a little laugh, 'without having to pay one.'

The business prospered so that Gustave, who I suspected was a man of low estate, was able to organise a similar *service confidentielle* from other hotels. Advertisements, she told me, now appeared regularly in all the leading newspapers offering 'gay companionship for lonely travellers on long tedious journeys. 57-35-23-24 will travel, write Box 69'. Gustave had to engage extra staff to meet these requirements.

All would have gone well for Yvonne if a strange chain of circumstances had not involved her emotionally in an adventure that eventually led to complications. With charming little-girl modesty, she told me how one night she happened to be in the *wagon-lit* of a distinguished diplomat, where she was probably not discussing the League of Nations or the Treaty of Versailles. She explained that he had the cutest white beard, parted in the centre, but strongly scented with attar of roses, a perfume to which she was allergic. She would not have refused the mission on this account, she explained, for Gustave had promised her a special present. It was clearly an important and delicate assignment because she had been instructed that in addition to her normal 'companionship service' she was to search through the man's bags and remove all the documents she could find.

While she continued her narrative I noticed that she kept peering out of the window. We were now deep in the mountains on this side of the Swiss Alps. Suddenly she cried dramatically: 'There . . . this is where it happened.' At the same time the great train swung inwards as it rounded a scimitar bend. 'This is where the train left the line and rolled over into the ravine . . . there.' And she gazed down and I could see that the poor girl was reliving the scene; and then her gaze travelled upwards into the mountains. 'There were great hot searing flames and the hiss of escaping steam. Then I remember nothing.' When she turned to me her eyes were wide and round and she sighed deeply.

Two miracles had happened that night. Firstly, a goatherd, hearing the crash and seeing the burning train from his mountain hut, hurriedly descended to the valley where, in the debris, he came upon Yvonne's naked body. She was unconscious but unhurt, and he carried her up to his hut. Two days later she recovered consciousness and saw the sun shining into the hut-door; but what interested her most was that the door was propped open by the diplomat's attaché case.

The goatherd, whose name was Axel, was a young and handsome creature and more representative of the wide open spaces than Gustave, she explained, for Axel was clean-shaven with fair hair, while her faithful Gustave was the narrow-faced type with a black line of a moustache and dark straight hair.

It was not surprising, therefore, that as Axel nursed her back to health in his primitive hut they should fall in love. A week of bliss was followed by one less blissful, and the time came when the bright lights and the music of Brussels (Axel played a wooden pipe) called to her.

She seemed to hesitate in her story as if there was something eluding her memory, then her eyes lit up and she said: 'Besides, I had got very tired of the smell of goat.'

As she continued I suddenly realised that the people I met would often tell me their stories. It seemed that I invited confidences. Was it possible that I had the magical gift, so necessary to a writer, of being a listener with my ears and my eyes?

'I don't suppose you've ever lived in a room for a fortnight with a herd of goats,' she said, looking at me enquiringly, as if she might be wrong. 'One morning when he'd gone to the village, I picked up the attaché case and left – without taking any of his money, which he kept hidden under the mattress.' She had found her way to the nearest station.

On her return to Brussels Gustave was overjoyed to see her, particularly as she had the attaché case, for he had given her and the case up for lost. The contents of the case proved to be of considerable value in the secret market to which Gustave took it. That afternoon he returned from the bank with a happy smile. He even invited her to dine at a cheap near-by restaurant before going back on duty at the hotel.

Yvonne thought occasionally of Axel, but the experience that she had undergone had been so bizarre that it soon took on the character of a dream. Business was brisk, and all might have been well if, one day, Gustave had not opened the door of the apartment to find Axel standing there, redolent of cognac and goat.

Explanations from Yvonne followed; for she had not told her adored Gustave the whole truth about her lost fortnight in the mountains. She now confessed all, and it was agreed that Yvonne should banish Axel to his mountains, where his goats must be missing him. But Axel had no intention of being banished, for he had already tasted some of the joys of civilisation, particularly in the form of alcohol. Yvonne pleaded with him; she even offered him money.

Stripped of enchantment, he haunted the flat, the street outside and the hotel. There in his shabby clothes he would appear in one door and disappear out of the other, having walked the length of the lounge and the *entresol* in search of Yvonne, usually 'under the influence'. Finally, Gustave warned her that unless Axel were careful his dead body would be found in an alley.

She sighed deeply: 'And do you know,' she said, 'it *was*; about a week later.' She frowned and remarked darkly: 'I've since wondered whether I shouldn't have warned him. In a foreign city a person has to be so careful, don't you think?'

'Are you still working?' I ventured.

'I'm on holiday,' she replied. 'Gustave said all work and no play makes Yvonne a dull girl.' She giggled. 'He's so thoughtful. I would like you to meet him some time when he is not too busy. We're going to be married any time now,' she added brightly. As she was preparing to leave I could not help asking her: 'Why did you tell me all this?'

'Well, if you want to know it was because you looked so sad and I hate to think of people being unhappy,' she said coyly. 'I thought that some of my luck might rub off. You see, I was so young and inexperienced when I first met Gustave, I often wonder what would have happened to me if I'd fallen into bad hands.'

In Vienna I was unable to obtain a room at the Bristol, but I managed to get in at the Grand. That evening, on the advice of the Countess Larisch, I took a box of Laranagas Coronas that I had bought from Trumper's in Curzon Street and presented them to Madame Sacher at her hotel. This delightful woman had been for two generations the Rosa Lewis of Vienna. She was the confidante of the grand dukes and an old friend of the Emperor Franz Joseph himself.

Her hotel stood close to the Opera House. It had a limited number of rooms, no American Bar and two restaurants on the ground floor, and was in many ways more musty and moth-eaten than the Cavendish. The old lady sat in the hall watching the arrival and departure of her guests as she chain-smoked the best cigars obtainable in Europe.

She was delighted with my present, and enquired with affection about Countess Larisch, a mutual friend, whom I had met with Eveleigh Nash. She had acted as a go-between in the ill-fated love affair of Marie Vetsera and Prince Rudolf. I now knew that

I would be given a table in the smaller restaurant which corresponded to being on the courtyard side of the Savoy Grill room in London. This is not something I would normally be interested in, never having been a table snob, but I had come to Vienna with the intention of picking up any promising business propositions, since the rate of exchange was heavily in favour of the pound and I might need this sort of build-up.

Indeed, the next morning I was greeted with the news that the crown had fallen to 50,000 to the pound. This meant that I was paying less than five shillings a night for my room and bathroom. For two days I enjoyed the income of a millionaire and spent it as money should be spent. I had the glorious opportunity of giving away hundreds of pounds that meant nothing to me. In a Cyranoesque way I have always loved the grand gesture, and for these two precious days I was given the opportunity of giving pleasure and extracting pleasure; of seeing eyes – old and tired, young and exquisite, all unbelieving – quicken and open wide in gratitude and astonishment.

I bought cigarette-cases and *bonbonnières*; the enamel work in Vienna was fabulous, and I was lucky enough to buy them before the prices rose.

At that time the Vienna of the *cafés chantants* and the *boîtes de nuit* was singing a charming waltz song – 'Nur Eine Nacht'. I was able to buy the English performing rights for a hundred pounds. There was another melody that I would have liked to buy, but it was not for sale, nor have I heard it since then. It was a song about a young man and a girl in a tram. He was making ardent love to her and, at the same time combining business with pleasure, he was transferring her purse to his pocket. The last line of the song ran: 'Ja, die wahre liebe war das nicht.' This could be translated: 'Now this could not have been genuine love.'

I spent wonderful days between Vienna and Semmering in the mountains and visited Mayerling where Marie and Rudolf consummated their love in a suicide pact. I had expected to find a small hunting-lodge; it turned out to be a reasonably sized country-house.

Charming as I found Vienna, it has never rivalled Paris in my affection. Paris is like a woman whom you never cease loving, however long you have been parted and however badly she has treated you. Whatever she has stolen out of your heart, she will never give it back.

My final business before leaving was to buy the agency for a wonderful violin that had just been put on the Austrian market with the strangely inappropriate name of the Tim. The cigarette-cases I had not given away I sold, on my return to London, to Astley's in Jermyn Street, and the *bonbonnières* to Asprey's and Finnigan's, making a hundred per cent profit on the deal. I kept for myself a cigarette-case which was plaited in three colours of gold with a cabochon emerald opening-catch. The Tim violin was not so successful, but not without interest.

I happened to see in *The Times* that Fritz Kreisler was in London. I knew that he would be at the Hyde Park Hotel, so I telephoned, asking his secretary whether he would give judge-ment on the newest violin made in Vienna. I was not surprised when an appointment was confirmed for the next day. Kreisler would never refuse to try out an instrument that had come direct from his beloved Vienna.

The next afternoon I had the extraordinary experience of hearing him play for me alone. He asked me what I would like, and I asked for his *Liebeslied*; and, of course, great artist that he was, once he had the violin in his hands he went on from one lovely composition to another. In his opinion it was, he said, a most excellent violin. This encounter should have spurred me on to go ahead with the marketing, but possibly the effort of selling the cigarette-cases and *bonbonnières* had been too much for me for I only know that I did nothing about it.

Months later I had a letter from the Customs in Southampton informing me that a hundred violins, addressed to me, were waiting to be cleared through the Customs. Alas, for all I know they are still there.

The waltz song I sold to Keith Prowse for two hundred pounds. It was introduced into a musical comedy at the Gaiety Theatre and sung by José Collins under the title 'Only one night'. Since then it has become a regular number in programme broadcasts all over the world, and it must have earned not less than fifty thousand pounds in royalties. I have composed music for films in collaboration with Frank Spencer; and as a member of the Performing Rights Society I know how efficiently they collect composers' royalties and how quickly they mount up. No performance escapes the net of this fantastic organisation, even when a film is playing in a flea-pit in the Middle West or a little mining town in Australia; they still collect the royalties.

It will be seen that my *métier* was, clearly, not business. Nonetheless, with three friends, Leslie Childers and Jasper Plowden and Walter Campbell, I started a business in St James's Street. We had acquired a fantastic machine for stamping out rubber heels. Leslie took premises on the first floor, but it was discovered at the eleventh hour that it would be necessary to build special supports from below to take the weight of the machine. This had to be done at considerable expense, because it involved overtime work on the building and overtime on the truck, which was even then on its way from Dumbarton with its precious cargo.

At last all was ready, the floor reinforced and the doorway below widened, together with the staircase. All arrangements had been made for the police to divert traffic, and in due course the great machine was unloaded and put in place. I find it difficult to remember what followed, but I seem to recall some sort of rise in the price of rubber or else a slump in heels, I forget which. Whatever it was, the machine never operated. Leslie, as managing director, spent two months of masterly inactivity, while Jasper and I spent most of our time with Paul Cremetti in his Maclean Galleries a few doors away, looking at his latest importations of Manet, Renoir, Monet or Sisley.

Suddenly our luck turned, and we were able to dispose of the machine to someone who wanted it for a completely different purpose from that for which it was intended.

The day for the removal of the machine arrived. The police had been informed, the traffic duly diverted, and that was the end of another business dream. Leslie was not always so lucky.

We used often to meet at the Guards Club in Brook Street. On one occasion at the club I was having a drink with Tim Nugent, who had befriended me when I first joined the regiment at a time when friendship was golden. The club secretary's assistant was a charming man who liked to look upon the wine when it was redder than it should have been. We had all been asked not to encourage him, so we were surprised to hear someone inviting him to have a drink in one of the alcoves along the passage that led to the dining-room. From one alcove, those in the next were audible, but not visible. We heard a persuasive voice insisting: 'Come on, you must have another whisky.'

'No, thank you.'

'I insist.'

'Well, if you insist, I suppose . . .'

'And a large one, too . . .'

'Well, if you insist . . .'

A moment later a waiter passed us with two large whiskies. Interested to know who was being so unwise as to push him faster in the direction he was already going, I got up and peered round the corner – only to discover, with an empty feeling in the pit of my stomach, that he was alone.

One day Leslie Childers met me in a state of jubilation. An uncle from whom he had great expectations had recently died and Leslie had received a letter from his solicitors in Edinburgh informing him that he had been mentioned in the will. They wished to check on Leslie's address before communicating the contents.

That night he organised a magnificent dinner at Claridge's to which he invited twenty-one of his friends. We duly saw him off on the night train to Scotland.

It was, alas, a chastened Leslie whom I saw a few days later, when he told me that all his uncle had left him was a set of ivory chessmen. He did not play chess, and said he was too old to learn.

Some years later Leslie dug the chessmen out of the attic and gave them away as a wedding present. Soon he was astonished to receive a letter of profuse thanks such as he had never received before: 'We cannot thank you enough for your most generous

F

present,' wrote the happy pair. 'Neither of us plays chess, but we have learned that the set you gave us is valued at a thousand pounds.'

Leslie was prepared to gamble on anything. It was reported that he once backed a man who had invented an eiderdown which, when it slipped off the bed, automatically sprang back. In many ways he was meticulous, and it was said that when he was on a diet he insisted on Robert Jackson supplying him with gruyère with king-sized holes in it.

Leslie had served in the Scots Guards in the First World War, and in 1939 he was anxious to join the M branch at the Admiralty, for which I was then working. I asked him whether he knew any admirals or other serving officers in the Navy, as my chief was influenced by a man's position in life, his service and social connections. Unfortunately, Leslie was unable to think of anyone at the time. But this little matter ended up satisfactorily, because a week later he wrote to me saying that he had just remembered his grandfather was First Lord of the Admiralty and he hoped it would help. In due course he joined us.

My final business venture began in Paris. This was a scheme to market a French tool of some sort which could be used on a lathe. As far as I can remember it was quite small, but seemed to weigh about a ton when carried in a dispatch case; and it was to be called the 'Ideal Tool-holder'.

I remember speaking to quite a few people about it. But one day, the weight of the dispatch-case having become intolerable, I left it in the cloakroom of the Monico Bar. When the management eventually came to open the case, they must have been extremely puzzled to know exactly what they had found, and to what use it could be put. No doubt in the course of time they discovered what the thing really was – something I'd never quite fathomed.

I2

The Demented City

IN the years just after the war I used often to visit Berlin.
Sometimes I would go by way of Ostend, where my old
friend Bagot Gray had opened a club. We had originally met
in Fleet Street, where he was working on a paper. Like myself,
he was a lost soul; and I was immediately charmed with his lazy
manner, his wit and dry humour.

His venture in Ostend would have been highly successful if he
had not, as usual, gambled away, in the early morning at the
Kursaal, the profits he had made at the club in the early hours of
the evening.

Loaded with champagne and lemonade, I would often visit an
artist friend who had a studio in the ill-famed Rue Courte. He
painted young naked girls: there was a decorative fashion for
nymphs on canvas murals at the time. We would play ridiculous
games or gamble in centimes, and there would be no more
painting or posing that day. With their modest eyes, their
innocent faces and their ribboned hair, even with their precocious
breasts, his models might have been sprites except for their
mischievous kissing tongues.

The artist and I would spend the rest of the night with Bagot
at the Kursaal if he was winning, or at the Royal Polo Bar when
he wanted to forget what he had lost. He was always either short
of a few hundred or else in the big money.

Bagot Gray once suggested that we should collaborate in a
farce he was writing; and so we went to work. It was produced
at the Duke of York's and ran (if it can be so expressed) for one

night. As Bagot said, it might have made theatrical history if a few days later it had not been beaten by a play that ran for one act only. Our play was called *Say When*, but we had the consolation of creating a record for the shortest critique when St John Ervine wrote in the *Observer* – 'Now.'

It was before one of the rehearsals of this unfortunate but enjoyable venture that I left part of the play on the District Railway. When I claimed it in Baker Street the man serving followed me into the street crying: 'You've left your umbrella on the counter.' To have lost an umbrella in a lost property office must have surely constituted yet another record.

To return to Berlin: I had many friends there, and when not travelling by Ostend I would drive from Paris through the golden autumn forests, a journey I never tired of. After Paris the life of Berlin – or the Village, as the diplomatic corps called it – was hard and brash.

The days could be lovely at Wannsee in the lakeside restaurants; and with Bodker of Reuters I used to burn the night away. At that time Berlin night-life had reached a point of depravity unequalled in any other European capital. There were cabarets where the women were dressed as men and the men as women: the Silhouette, the Taverna and the Jockey Club were the most popular. In the Friedrichstrasse, when one was accosted, it might, quite probably, be by a man in woman's clothes; in one of the transvestite clubs it was the fashion for these unhappy creatures to be garbed as youthful Queen Victorias, in crinolines and long frilly drawers. Once, with my brother-in-law, we watched a lovely girl in a cabaret act; when I invited her to our table, we found that the exquisite creature who had enchanted me was a young boy from Charlottenburg.

There were houses where the women were dressed as little girls and little girls as women; others masqueraded as meek nuns or were arrayed in bridal gowns freshly sprinkled with confetti; there were mothers-and-daughters and sisters-and-brothers: every fantasy was catered for. There were kinky establishments for sadists and masochists, equipped with ingenious instruments of torture, scourges and whips of great sophistication, an array of handcuffs from every country, and a collection of black velvet masks for those who desired anonymity.

I made a friend in the police who took me to many of the bars habitually used by the criminal classes and tolerated for the convenience of the Polizei, who could thus keep in touch with their clients. This fraternisation of police and predators I never found wholly uncongenial; it was certainly preferable to the philistine and unlovely gang of financiers and *Schieber* who infested the doomed and demented city.

My police friend told me that the German military collapse of 1918 – the so-called *Dolchstoss im Rücken* – was attended by a widespread moral breakdown: women of the now impoverished middle and professional classes were selling themselves for bars of chocolate or cakes of soap.

This unfair amateur competition aroused great indignation among the professional prostitutes, *Strassenmädchen* and holders of the 'Yellow ticket'. A mass-meeting was held, resolutions were passed and a deputation of veterans marched to police headquarters to lodge a petition demanding protection against this 'dilution of labour'.

A rewarding evening could certainly be spent in these *Nachtlokale* by anyone interested in the odder manifestations of our common sensuality.

In the early twenties of the ill-fated Weimar Republic I came across my friend Patrick Kirwan. He too shared my fascinated interest in this bizarre underworld and had readily accepted an invitation by a high-ranking police official to make a tour of Hamburg's notorious Reeperbahn and Wasserkante, and with the morning hours they had wound up in a *Bierkeller* in the St Pauli district, a subterranean dockside rendezvous for *warme Brüder* and homosexual criminals. The prettily rouged waiters were dressed as sailor-boys with deep-plunging neck-lines and hip-hugging bell-bottoms. Between prancing around with the *Bier* and *Schnapps* they danced the Black Bottom with ugly muscular thugs to the deafening music of an amplified three-piece band.

Suddenly a hush fell on the company and all looked to the head of the stairway leading down from street-level. A fantastic figure stood framed in the entrance: a huge middle-aged man in a curly blonde wig, breathlessly corseted and with the train of his sequined satin Edwardian evening gown draped over his brawny kid-gloved forearm. He was fanning the brute hair on his chest (over which flowed a glittering diamond-and-emerald *rivière*) with a fistful of ostrich plumes.

His raddled cheeks were pendulous and a bluish five-o'clock shadow bristled beneath pink powder. Wobbling in king-size satin court-shoes he descended the stairs to where the bugger-boys stood bowing low.

'Baron von —' whispered the police official. 'Very important in the Foreign Office – comes here for a little relaxation – one of my dearest friends.'

Smiling a little, the police official took out a neat compact and, after a quick dab at both cheeks, lipsticked himself expertly, baring his teeth in a scrutinising snarl before hiding them again behind the cutest cupid's-bow. The three-piece band struck up a Viennese waltz.

'Excuse me, please,' said the police official and he floated away to beg the pleasure of a dance of his huge ecstatic Freundin. Pat, like myself, had served in Flanders, while still in his teens, and twice been wounded. But although he came of a long line of Irish professional soldiers he was so appalled by the wanton slaughter of the trenches and disgusted by the philistinism of the savage capitalist society that awaited the warrior from the wars returning that he turned communist and professional revolutionary. At this time, being some kind of a linguist, he was working on clandestine publications under the direction of the brilliant but unwashed Russian conspirator and journalist Karl Radek.

Unlike myself, who had gained a faith in the war, Pat had lost his; which was probably why he embraced so eagerly and violently the Marxist substitute for the doctrines of Mother Church. But when the death of Lenin and the decline of Trotsky was followed by the seizure of power by Stalin he realised that he had taken to his heart, not the fair genius of *liberté, égalité et fraternité*, but a monstrous spectre of famine, tyranny and spiritual death.

This swift and second loss of faith drove him to sit all day in a squalid café off the Friedrichstrasse cooling his elbows on a marble-topped table and consuming a throat-burning procession of brandies. Together we drank our way to sanity out of our private and particular griefs. Between drinks his head would be couched in a sleeping attitude on his arms: then suddenly he would come to life and, raising a clenched fist, would shout, in ringing tones, 'Too long have I been the anvil.' His head would then resume its former position until the arrival of a fresh drink automatically aroused him; and then he would straighten up, eyes flashing and clenched fist once more upraised, his voice echoing once again through the café, 'Now I will be the hammer.' The stirring words faded, his head slumped forward and assumed its sleeping position, until the reappearance of another drink sparked off a repetition of the macabre scene. As this was a quotation from Goethe it was listened to with respectful attention.

Sometimes I could persuade him to sing the lovely, sad song of the Irish Famine in his clear baritone, with his fine head thrown back and his dark eyes flashing. The café would be suddenly hushed to silence, the waiter standing motionless, the customers' conversation dying away to a whisper.

> Oh the praties they are small
> Over here, over here. . . .
> Oh, the praties they are small
> And we dug them in the fall
> And we ate them coats and all
> Full of fear. . . .

By the time he had reached the last verse there was hardly a dry eye among the sentimental Germans, for even those who did not understand could divine the sincerity and mourning in the old lament.

> I wish that we were geese
> Night till morn, night till morn,
> I wish that we were geese,
> For they spend their days in peace.
> To the hour of their decease
> Eating corn, eating corn. . . .
>
> We're down into the dust
> Over here, over here,
> We're down into the dust
> But our faith in God we trust
> He'll feed us with a crust.
> Over here, over here.

Though we didn't know it Pat's name and number, even then, was listed for liquidation. He was invited by his immediate superior, a well-known American comrade, to go for a ride in a *Droschke* round the Tiergarten, as the man wished to have a private talk with him. As they drove down the Siegesallee, that ghastly collection of heroic Hohenzollern effigies now happily destroyed, the American told Pat he was being posted to Moscow to work in the Comintern. Then he stopped the *Droschke* and, almost compassionately, handed Pat an apple. Wondering, Pat raised it to his nostrils; but it evoked no memories of laughing girls in sunlit orchards. It smelled of death. That night he headed not for Moscow but London.

There, almost inadvertently, a party 'Bonze' blurted out that he had been too open in his denunciations of Stalin; it was feared that he might defect and tell what he knew. He need not have worried. Pat had a fine contempt for the shabby army of literary ex-communists: 'When you've loved a woman you don't write dirt about her; even though she was a whore and a bitch.'

There was the other side of Pat, which loved to be with me under the star-reflecting chandeliers of the great international restaurants or living a life of ease and reading in the green twilight of tapestry-hung rooms. He appeared to regard life as he would a triptych mirror where he could study the reflection from every angle. He had the great art of mixing sadness with a zest for enjoyment, accompanied by a first-class mind and the gift of being able to break down a problem, so that it became already half solved. He is the only man I have ever known who was not only able to sum up a person correctly, but also to see him as he appeared to himself. These gifts made him an ideal companion for a person of my temperament.

Years later I was best man at his marriage to Celia, one of the Paget twins, who were, at that time, the toast of fashionable London. He had already given up novels and belles-lettres and, not without a certain amusement, was writing some of the most successful original films for Korda, and wartime *Evening Standard* leaders for Lord Beaverbrook.

As we dined at the Connaught after the wedding reception at Claridge's it was almost impossible to realise that this was the same man who had once been a habitué of seedy revolutionary hang-outs, with a murderous committee awaiting his arrival in Moscow.

One day in Berlin I visited Magnus Hirschfeld's museum. This doctor was the leading authority on all off-beat sexual matters. He had a library with the most catholic collection of erotica in the world. In addition he had assembled a startling series of photographs, acquired in the course of his untiring researches. I had a letter of introduction so I was allowed to see everything. The library was so extensive that I was introduced to a young man to guide me round, and to show me everything of interest that could be seen in a single afternoon.

The young man behaved throughout my visit, as one would expect, very politely, but as we were leaving he surprised me by taking my hand and running it over his cheeks and chin. This, he explained, was to demonstrate how all the natural growth of hair had been electrically removed. I suppose that was reasonable enough, but I was taken completely by surprise when I felt the imprint of his lips on my hand before he released it. Nor did I then realise the difficulty I would have in scrubbing the lipstick off on my return to the Adlon.

F2

I learned afterwards from Oswald Hafenrichter, who edited the Oscar-winning film, *The Third Man*, and was working at UFA films in Berlin at the same time, that the poor devil was well known as a transvestite and committed suicide when Hitler decreed all Germans should be 'normal like himself'.

On another evening in Berlin, Fritz, the perfect hotel-valet, had as usual laid out my evening clothes. On a side-table was my tray of hors d'œuvres and a specially dry Martini. My bath had been drawn to exactly the right temperature, my evening-studs were lined up on the dressing-table next to my gleaming silver brushes; and into a slender glass, just big enough to hold a flower, he had remembered to put a Venetian-red carnation.

In the hotel bar there was the usual bunch of *monde* and *demi-monde*, drinking and gossiping. I knew most of the newspapermen. I joined them for a short time and then made my escape, for in their company the drinks were too cold, too strong and too frequent, and I was feeling sufficiently tolerant to endure my own company that evening.

After an excellent dinner in the restaurant I remembered a cabaret that Bodker of Reuters had recommended. 'You should go to the Kazbec if you want to be alone without being lonely.' And that was exactly how I felt.

I found my way to the place. As the door swung open I was assailed by the reek of stale cigar smoke, cheap perfume and perspiring bodies when I should have recognised the stench of death by murder.

Around the dance floor and lighting the room were glittering globes like enormous circular diamonds with mirrored facets that caught and reflected the light as they revolved. Occasionally they opened to reveal small fountains of water tinted in green and blue and red. There were telephones on each table, each one bearing a number illuminated in red. There were girls and more girls, and the whole operation was clearly intended to induce a friendly *Stimmung* – to put it mildly.

I found a table in a corner away from the dance-floor. At the next table an elderly German was engaged in an animated conversation. He was speaking slowly and persuasively. Then

the telephone at my table rang and a strangely uneasy pre-
monition filled me as I lifted the receiver.

'Hello, do you like to dance?' There was an invitation in the
voice. 'It is sometimes pleasanter to dance than to talk.'

'You seem to have danced yourself away from school,' I
replied, because it was unmistakably the voice of a very young
girl.

'Possibly. . . .'

The sweet strains of 'An der schönen blauen Donau' were
coming from the orchestra.

'You are English?' she continued. 'Only an Englishman could
come here *im Frack*.' There was a little laugh. 'Your countrymen
will go to Paradise dressed in their black ties.'

'But, supposing this is Paradise,' I answered. 'Paradise is only
where you find happiness, and . . . angels.'

There was a pause and then the low sweet voice continued:
'If there are angels here, we have left our haloes at home . . .'

'With your dolls?'

There was a gurgle of laughter.

'You cannot judge my age from my voice. It is my thoughts
that you must read.' I detected a slight note of bitterness.

'I was taught that it was rude to read people's thoughts.'

'Then perhaps I shall enjoy talking to you,' she answered.
'You should ask me whether I come here often. Oh yes, that is
always the first question.'

'I'm certain that you haven't been coming here very long.'

What was she like, the possessor of this lovely voice? I was
only faintly interested in what she was saying; it was like
listening to a beautiful voice singing in an unknown language.
All I wanted to do was listen.

'Not for long,' said the voice in a whisper. 'Not for long,' she
repeated, 'because . . .' She hesitated. 'Father forbade me to
come here.'

'And your mother?'

'My mother died during the war. . . . She was sick and we
were poor, if you understand the meaning of the word. Father
was a soldier, then, later, a porter at a foreign embassy.'

It was an amazing voice, dark and warm, if a voice can be described in these terms; and though it was fresh and youthful, it was at the same time, composed, fully composed. It contained certain cadences that I had heard before in no other human voice. I sat spellbound, allowing its caressing intonations to flow over and completely possess me.

'He was afraid of pleasure. . . . He was afraid of everything when it concerned me. And to be afraid of pleasure . . .' She drew in her breath sharply. 'It is dangerous to be afraid of pleasure.'

The voice was not only melodious, it was compulsively interesting with its ever-changing tones; yet underlying all there was a strange note of sadness.

'It is dangerous to be afraid of pleasure,' she repeated, and then I was conscious of something sinister. There were things she told me tenderly with the words hardly above a whisper, childhood stories – a short childhood it must have been; she told me of the things which gave her pleasure and in the shadowed background there stalked, limping, the angry figure of her father, remote and inflexible, with his artificial leg, ill-fitting and increasing his natural irritability, a frustrated non-commissioned officer, with no soldiers to bully.

'For other girls there were the "flicks", parties, swimming and dancing; for me nothing, except . . . those sad walks beside the Spree canal alone with him, talking of the Kaiser and the pre-war Germany and his exploits on the Somme, shouting his stories to the bargemen until he drove them below decks. Every day we would take our walk, and always I would see the men escaping below when they saw us approaching the quayside. Sometimes they would loosen the warps and steer midstream to avoid us, but my father would tempt them back with tobacco and cigars. It seemed that he spoke always of what others wanted to forget.'

The picture rose vividly to my mind, the lame man stalking the quayside, flooding the evening with his interminable soldier's tales. And all the time watching with one eye the girl at his side, clutching her arm occasionally and pulling her forward when the speed of the barges quickened.

It was difficult to tell whether she was telling the truth. To make truth sound true it is often necessary to embroider it with fiction, as if to magnify the gleam of truth.

'It was not often that I was out of his sight, but there were times when his leg was too painful and I had to go alone to buy our provisions.' For a moment she was silent and I had left the river and was back in the cabaret with the white tablecloth and the slender black bottle of hock in its ice-bucket. Then the soft voice started speaking again.

'Why am I telling you all this?'

'Because you know I am interested.'

'Because your voice is gentle, or because you're a stranger who'll forget or because I feel that you understand things good and bad. . . . This is a cabaret confessional,' she whispered.

I waited.

'One evening, because things happen to lonely people, a girl-friend stopped me in the street and told me that there was a man who wanted to know me.'

'You met him?'

'Yes, and why not? It was the first time that anyone had wanted to know me. So that very evening as it was getting dark I slipped away from father; he shouted to me from the quayside, and he tried to catch me, but with his artificial leg . . . you understand? He wasn't quick enough.'

'And the man?' I asked. She must have shrugged her shoulders.

'Oh, the man, he was old but he was kind.' She paused for a moment and the silence was like a sigh. 'When I returned home my father beat me.'

It was possible that the rich laughter in her voice was to hide her shame at being punished, for I seemed to detect a note of bravado as she added: 'Of course, I was used to that, but please believe me' – now the voice was pleading – 'before that there'd been no occasion to beat me.'

'And the next time?'

'I escaped again and met the man, and later at the hotel he gave me money, much money. Had I not suffered to please him? He knew because he'd seen the scars on my body. He showed me

how to hide the money in the top of my stocking. That night my
father thrashed me again – this time I felt the buckle-end of his
belt. After that I was a prisoner. All day he stayed with me,
watching me, and when we walked the river-bank in the twilight
his hand clutched my belt in his iron grip, but when he descended
the steps to the water's edge, it was I who always had to hold
him because the steps were slippery.'

When she spoke again it was in a whisper, though every word
was distinct. And it was to be the last time that I was to hear the
deathly beauty of that voice.

'Last night father slipped . . . and with his artificial leg . . .
poor Father! No one could expect him to swim.'

I could hear her frightened breathing, for she knew that she
had *spoken* – the need to confess had been too strong. Gently I
hung up the receiver and reached for my bill.

Outside, morning was mantling the skies over the Kurfürsten-
damm; broad red spirals, swept by the winds, were fading in the
light of the approaching day and the warm smell of fresh bread
was beginning to spread through the city.

On a later visit to Germany I had a brief glimpse of what was
in store. When the hotel-valet brought my rolls and coffee and a
freshly pressed suit in the morning, his usually smiling face was
glum. 'Stresemann died last night,' he announced. 'Now the
trouble will begin.'

From my hotel window I could look down onto the garden.
I saw a parade of page-boys lined up for inspection by an under-
manager. At a harsh word of command they leapt to attention.
As the parade proceeded each boy turned about, faced front
again and presented his finger-nails for inspection.

One was reprimanded for a dull or missing button; another
appeared to have only one white glove under his epaulette.
Names were taken and the parade dismissed. The under-manager
stood in his black coat and striped trousers at attention for a
moment. But it was a soldier in the guise of a civilian who
marched off. He might as well have been dressed in uniform
himself.

13

Nichevo, Tovarich

THE urge to travel farther afield was beginning to take possession of me. I also realised that I was too selfish ever to adjust myself to the mutual give-and-take of married life and the discipline of office-hours.

For me the long honeymoon was over; the flood of happy-sad memories was overlaid with an increasing sense of economic servitude and spiritual death. I decided that only toil in the form of manual work or constant travel could bring me a sense of freedom. I had grown to manhood in time of war, and to experience war is to lose all sense of reality. As I look back over the years this hunger for reality – towards which unconsciously I must have been reaching – is the only justification I can offer for my selfish escapism.

I went to see Sir Godfrey Thomas at the Foreign Office, but although I had made one journey already as a King's Messenger they were up to strength; besides which, I was, it appeared, still too young even to go on the waiting list. I had applied for a visa to visit Russia. Now this had come through; it was as if fate was directing my steps. Whatever decision I finally took, I had to visit Russia before I did anything else. This might be my first lesson in how the other half of the world lived.

Soon I was travelling on the broad-gauge Red Arrow, returning to Leningrad after a visit to Moscow. That evening, with two foreign correspondents, I had watched a dress-rehearsal of *Prince Igor* at the Bolshoi Theatre. The stalls seemed to be empty save for the three of us sharing the same bottle of vodka. Suddenly there was light, sound, colour and movement. The

curtain had risen on the great encampment of the wild Polovtsi.
The air that drifted across the footlights was charged with the
strange musty smell of chiffon and oriental brocade, mixed with
the exciting animal stench of fur and the tang of size on new-
painted scenery. Never have I smelt more magnificent smells or
savoured so magnificent a sense of barbaric splendour, enriched
by Borodin's lovely music.

I will never forget the first part of that evening for its beauty,
nor the second for its ugliness.

I boarded the train immediately after the rehearsal, hoping for
a long night in which to sleep off the effects of the vodka. I was
already comfortably bedded in the upper berth of the compartment when the door opened and the occupant of the lower
berth, a Russian officer, entered. Gradually the compartment
became clouded with the acrid smoke and foul smell of the
mahorka cigarettes he was smoking. I leaned over and opened the
window. He proceeded to close it. Defiantly I opened it again.

No word passed between us. He stood watching me closely
with expressionless oriental eyes. Then, slowly, he took his
revolver out and with great deliberation laid it on the mirror-
shelf beyond my reach. Once more he closed the window. The
train had left the outskirts of Moscow. He was standing swaying
beside the window gazing out, for now the train was slowing to
a halt. We were in a country station. I could see horses with high
wooden collars harnessed to country carts and a group of tall,
bearded men gazing upwards vacantly at the train. They stood
motionless, yet clearly defined in the white light of a harvest-
moon.

Now the train was on the move again, gathering speed. The
officer was removing his uniform jacket and rolling up his shirt
sleeve. From his case he produced a hypodermic which he
charged from a small ampoule. This done, he held it up to the
light. Satisfied with what he saw, he drove the needle with
unhesitating aim into the antecubital vein that ran like a blue
streak down his forearm.

Already I felt physically sick with the heat in the compartment
and the nauseating stench of *mahorka*, but this last action was

more than I could stand. To climb from my sleeper I had to turn my back to him. This done with as much deliberation as I could summon, I put on my dressing-gown. Still his hand remained resting on the revolver and now when I turned to face him there was a smirk on his face as he watched me unlock the door. I found the car-attendant and explained what had happened as best I could in a mixture of English, French and mime. He immediately locked the officer in the compartment and fixed me up in his own berth.

Next morning my little Soviet guide, Tanya, met me at the station, as no doubt she had been instructed. I told her what had happened on the train. She listened to me seriously with a grey-eyed, level gaze.

'That is bad,' she said, shrugging her coat more firmly on her shoulders; for she always wore it cavalry style.

'That is bad,' she repeated.

'Bad for who?' I asked.

As we watched the military escort march him off I felt her hand on my arm. 'When it is proved against him he will be punished as an enemy of the state.' Her small oval face showed grave anxiety.

At that time there was no future for an enemy of the state. I realised that I had brought death or worse to a man for no better reason than that he smoked *mahorka* cigarettes and sought forgetfulness in dreams.

'Nichevo, tovarich,' she whispered, 'nichevo.'

I remembered my first meeting with her in the Hotel Astoria immediately on my arrival in Leningrad. It was in the Torgsin store off the central hall. An exquisite little Persian rug had caught my attention. I had stopped to run my hand over its silky surface, when I realised someone was beside me and I glanced round cautiously.

'You like Persian rugs?' she asked.

'It isn't often one sees two such beautiful things at the same moment.'

'I'm a guide,' the girl remarked gravely.

'Are there any more like you where you come from?' I asked.

She was the first well-groomed girl I had seen in Russia. Moreover she was beautiful in a European way; and looked capable of kissing her jewellery or being angry at leaving her hand-mirror at home.

'I don't come from anywhere,' she answered.

'Where are you going to, then?' I enquired.

'Nowhere in particular.'

'That's where I was going, so we might as well go there together.'

From then on she was with me almost continually, taking me to places I did not want to visit and showing me things I had no wish to see. I was not so foolish as to think that this first meeting beside the little Persian rug had been by chance. She had obviously been detailed to be my guide.

There were times when I even believed that I was reasonably in love with her, for under the hard shell of the Komsomol there existed a woman, a lovely woman, searching instinctively for the rich silks and satins of life. Yet she loved Russia and had she suspected me of being an enemy I believe she would have killed me, even with a kiss. She was quite prepared to liquidate the bourgeoisie single-handed, and although I was an ordinary man with an unquenchable thirst for the good things in life, to her I represented independence, something she secretly craved for. I believe that in the short time I knew her she elevated me to a mystical state of *independent man*, merely because I had seen the sun rise and fall beyond her prison-world. To her I represented life beyond the horizon, an obscure future that she was never likely to share with anyone, even with someone she might one day love. I was a glimpse into a life that could never be more than part of her dreams.

She could be very charming, particularly when she chose to be serious and comradely and when I would have none of it; for in a romantic way, I believed more in love than in friendship with a woman. I tried to persuade her that some kind of love for each particular period of everyone's life was a necessity, not, as she pretended, a useless luxury, a bourgeois emotion. It seemed to me, in my European way, unreasonable that I should not be allowed to love, at least temporarily, a girl whose company I enjoyed so much.

There was the moment in my hotel when I surprised her lying on my bed with the sheets pushed down to her feet. She was wearing a pair of my red silk pyjamas, which on her were so big that the jacket had slipped away from one ivory shoulder, while the other arm was raised to her head so that the hand was hidden in a dark cluster of curls.

She could pretend anything – that was an important part of her training. Now she was pretending to be asleep, but I knew that she was watching me under her lashes, because I could see the narrow gleam of metallic grey that betrayed her.

'You evade nothing by pretending,' I said, with all the experience of a born escapist.

She opened her eyes wide, with that level gaze she could assume when she wished to mislead me.

'You're watching me, *tovarich*, when it is I who should be watching you.'

She moved each hand sleepily over her breasts in a circular movement and closed her eyes. A little while later she was genuinely asleep, breathing evenly like a child, dreaming her dreams of blast-furnaces, saw-mills, tractors and cement-mixers, or whatever a Russian girl dreams about.

I was reminded that I had my own troubles that were not dreams. At that time it was necessary for foreigners on entering Russia to declare the amount of pounds, dollars, francs, etc., that they were carrying. We were encouraged to spend our *valuta* or foreign currency at Torgsin stores, but roubles were also necessary for outside spending, and this Russian money was supplied at a ridiculously low government exchange-rate. The transactions were then recorded on a receipt-note. Anything purchased during our visit to Russia we had to declare on leaving and if it was in roubles we had to show the receipted bill.

Shortly after arriving in Russia I had formed a black exchange contact. There were certain people prepared to give you wads of roubles for foreign currency, though they risked their lives for it. Because of this I was able to buy a magnificent Persian-lamb coat,

black as night, with shining skins of short close-curling fur. At
the legal government rate of exchange it would have cost about
£1000. I had bought it for less than £250, but I had still to get it
out of the country. Already I too had become an enemy of the
state.

My friend from whom I obtained the roubles to buy the coat
was a charming Jewish musician who played with the Leningrad
State Orchestra. As I said good-bye to him a few weeks later
I little knew that I was destined to betray him into the hands of
those he most feared.

On my return from Russia I wrote a book *Gun Cotton goes to
Russia*. It was largely fictional, and it described this particular
visit to Russia without the tragic cross-currents that defaced it.
In my manuscript I mentioned Ivanov and our illegal business
transaction, intending to substitute a fictitious name in the final
proof-copy. Unfortunately, I then went unexpectedly to South
America and it was some months before I returned. To my
everlasting shame and regret I had forgotten to change his name
when I passed the proof. When I returned, the book was already
on sale and it was only after a few weeks that the news reached
me that he had been arrested by the G.P.U. and the rest was
silence.

Three men were to go to their deaths through their ill-fated
meetings with me. Through the years I can still hear Tanya's
whispered '*Nichevo, tovarich, nichevo.*'

One evening, because I thought that what I had to do was
none of her business, it was necessary to evade her. My uncle
Maurice, many years previously, had married Princess Natasha
Gregoriev. The marriage had taken place in St Petersburg, as it
was then known, but only after the greatest difficulty because the
civil authorities had asked him to produce documents to prove
he was not already married. This was quite impossible to do.
Even in those days Russia was obsessed with the importance of
papers and strangled in red-tape. Eventually, and only because
Aunt Nata's uncle was Governor of Kronstadt and stood
guarantor, would they accept Maurice's word of honour that he
was a bachelor.

Now, before leaving London, Nata had made me promise to try to contact her sisters, who, she believed, might still be living in their old town house in the Avenue Garde de Cheval. The difficulty I was faced with was how to find my way there without making enquiries. It was impossible for me even to read the street names in the Russian lettering, even had I known the district in which to look.

Fortunately, in the hall of the hotel I discovered under a piece of plate glass on the enquiry desk a complete map of the city, and, by chance, my eyes immediately fell on the name of the avenue, probably because, as I should have guessed, it was printed in French. Leningrad at that period was an uncomfortable place for foreigners, for one was conscious of being under observation from the moment one left the privacy of the bedroom. It was a city of watchers and listeners. I have always had a sense of location and, taking a roundabout route, preceded by my own shadow, I eventually arrived at the Avenue Garde de Cheval. It proved to be a broad avenue with a line of trees down the centre. This was the old residential section of Leningrad. There were tall blocks of houses on my right, bordered by the canal. Behind me was the distant, slender, golden spire of the Admiralty. A short distance away was the Palace of Labour and, on the left, the dark façade of the Post Office.

I was, at last, able to locate the house. The sisters were established in one room of their old home and I was able to give them Nata's letters. They told me enough of the lives they led to convince me that my visit was endangering them should it become known. During the time I was there a young girl cousin stood at the door to make sure that no one was listening outside.

When I eventually left I hugged the shadow of the houses, for I had no wish that we should all undergo cross-examination under Klieg lamps with a pulse-register on my wrist; and then be directed down a dark passage followed by someone with a heavy, silenced revolver in his hand and carpet slippers on his feet. At that time typhus was one of the few fevers that left its victims with a red mark at the back of the skull about the size of a bullet from a gun fired at short range.

I was relieved when I got clear of the avenue and the dark doorways that seemed to harbour waiting figures. As in a Rembrandt, the most interesting effects were due to the absence of light. Threatening clouds were sailing across a pale moon when I at last found my way to the Yussupoff Palace. This was a place that I was determined to see, and it was not included in the official sight-seeing tours. There I leaned over the embankment parapet and gazed into the canal. A few huddled figures lay like black shadows on the benches behind me.

The water of the canal stretched like a silver ribbon, reflecting the swift-moving clouds on its surface. The street was silent. Behind me stood the heavy pillars that fronted the long, low Yussupoff Palace. Moonbeams glinted palely on the iron bars that faced the windows of the cellar. It was here that Rasputin, the enemy of his country in 1916, was assassinated in the name of Holy Russia by Prince Felix Yussupoff. The side door showed black and forbidding. It was through this doorway that the monk's cyanide-poisoned, counter-poisoned, and re-poisoned, bullet-ridden body was dragged.

The executioners jettisoned the body in the canal, higher up beyond the bridge, so that no suspicion would fall on the palace. They broke the ice and pushed the body under, and even then, with the 'corpse' submerged, the hands of the half-dead man kept clawing at the ice until they stamped them under.

Back at the hotel, at the highest bar I had ever seen, I climbed on to a stool. An American next to me remarked: 'Evening, friend. Been having a look round? Tell me, what makes them tick? Here they treat every individual child as a physical-psychical personality, not as a biological organism.'

'Are their methods pedagogical or merely prophylactical?' I asked innocently, for one of the barmaids had approached.

'Psycho-neurological, I'd say,' he replied.

'Well, well. In that case I'll have a vodka, a large one, and another one on the side, please.'

The barmaid was listening with interest. If these hotel girls were employed as agents, espionage was taking a turn for the better. The Russian authorities were no fools: smiles like theirs and laughing eyes so full of meaning could learn far more than the rat-hole spies and clumsy shadowers of the old régime. The American and I, however, had nothing to impart except what drinks we wished her to serve. We foreigners soon learned to keep our thoughts to ourselves.

One day Tanya took me to Tsarskoe Selo, a few miles out of the city. The palace had been preserved as a museum. Everything was as the imperial family had left it on the night of their departure on the journey that led to death.

The royal apartments comprised a number of small rooms opening off a long corridor. In the nursery the children's toys were scattered about the floor. In the Tsar's bedroom I saw his suits and uniforms hanging up and his brushes on his dressing table.

The intention of the government was to illustrate the bourgeois existence of the Tsar of all Tsars and his family. An open book was on a bedside table in his room. I could not resist the temptation to step over the cord stretched as a barrier across the room. Without touching the book I saw that it was the *Pools of Silence* by de Vere Stacpoole. On my return to England I wrote to him informing him that probably the last book on earth to be read by the Tsar was his story of the Belgian atrocities in the Congo. In due course I received an invitation to visit him in Somerset.

Back in the hotel the bar was crowded with tourists waiting like sheep for their shepherdesses. Most of them were enthusiastic about everything that had been shown to them. Personally, I was not particularly interested in the political significance of what was taking place, nor was I concerned about the success or failure of the Five Year Plan. In my lazy way I was interested only in the people and their reactions to what they were doing and what was being done to them. That is not to say I was not excited by the strangeness of this new world through which I was being so adroitly guided by Tanya, with few chances of escape.

There was one evening in Moscow when, unaccompanied, I saw Red Square and the great citadel of the Kremlin for the first time. The long wall on one side of the square had recently been painted white. Above it the gilded domes and spires pierced the twilight sky. The Kremlin side of the square was flood-lit. Lenin's tomb was then a small structure of polished red stone, but in spite of its squat appearance there was a simple beauty about it. Over the Kremlin the lazily flapping Soviet flag made a splash of red in the draining light. On my left the fantastic façade of St Basil's Cathedral lifted its phallic turrets and breast-like domes, the cross of Christianity crowning its highest point. Across the square the Tsarist eagles still perched on the great gates.

It began to rain. While I was absorbed in my surroundings, my attention was diverted to a shabby-looking individual standing near the queue outside the tomb. The unhurried signal the man had made was unmistakable. I followed him because that was what I had to do. The rain was now splashing hard on the pavements and filling the gutters. I kept the hunched figure at a reasonable distance.

Presently, in a narrow street off Maroseika he turned sharply into a doorway and glanced back. A street lamp at the corner threw a lurid circle of light. It looked as if we had not been tailed.

Cautiously, I followed him up two flights of stairs. The darkness was tainted with the stench of old clothes and unwashed bodies. We entered a room: a dim light, thrown by a tallow candle, flickered in a corner. Here the smell of used-up air and poor people was even more pungent. I groped for my pipe. Several mattresses edged the sweating walls.

'That's mine,' the man said in English, pointing into the shadows. 'The others are used by men who come in at all times, snatch a few hours' sleep, then move on. The building is condemned, but there's a man below who's acquired sort of squatter's rights and collects a few kopecks when he's lucky.' His pale eyes were shining in a face drained of colour.

'One can get used to anything.' He handed me a sheaf of papers which he had concealed under his mattress. It was only later that I realised what a neatly written memorandum he had compiled of the information he wished to impart. All concerned happenings peculiar to that period of communist Russia's history, and I was to deliver them to the Russian Section at the Foreign Office.

'There's lots that isn't in here,' he said. 'Now this is for your memory.' For a long time he whispered eagerly. To this day I can still remember some of the things this strange pedlar of information told me. It was a long time since he had gone to sleep with the darkness and awakened with the light, for he lived in a twilight world of hushed whispers and strange happenings.

'Don't think I haven't my dreams,' he said. 'A bath, clean linen, dinner, good wine and a cigar.'

'Is that impossible?'

'For me it's impossible,' he replied. 'A man with no papers in this country must live in the shadows, even when he has money.' He tapped his shabby coat. 'The F.O. pay so little for information. They are very mean. The Germans pay better, but I give them only the carcass, after our people have eaten the meat. Go now, and many thanks. Watch your step.'

I never knew whether he was officially employed or whether he was a free-lance purveyor of information, of which there were many, I was told, in Russia. Nor was I ever to see him again, though from time to time I enquired about him without success from those to whom I eventually delivered his notes and from others who might be expected to know. In that period, people in Russia without papers died very quietly, with hardly a scream. It was a period of history when it was said that people cried very little. The colour just passed out of their eyes.

As I stepped out into the street a man was standing a few yards away. He beckoned me. I could hardly avoid him, for he was standing where I had to pass. Suddenly, he put out a pudgy hand intending, I imagine, to grab my arm. There was the strong reek of spirits about him, and it was obvious that he had been drinking. He was standing at the top of a flight of stairs that led down to a sort of basement. I made only the gentlest movement. I must have caught him off balance. It happened like a film in slow motion. I even had time to notice the fleshy face perspiring

and the lids of eyes that were lashless and the surprised expression
as he muttered something in Russian, then he fell backwards to
the basement, bulkily and silently like a sack of flour. He lay
silent and unmoving.

I can give no explanation for this sombre incident, but all
foreigners visiting Russia at that time were shadowed. Whether
the man intended questioning me about the house I had just left
or whether he was a simple drunk I couldn't tell. What I do know
is that back at the hotel, in the bathroom, I brought up the
dinner that I had previously enjoyed.

The following day was spent with Tanya and a party of
tourists inspecting factories and new workers' flats. After the
incidents of the previous night I was like a man with a hangover;
and, what was worse, I was afraid, afraid as a man can be afraid
only in Russia.

That evening I was anxious to look over the wharf from which
my ship was due to leave next morning. To take the roundabout
route in order to throw off trackers had become habitual. And I
was becoming quite expert at it, except that one could never be
certain that the man thrown off had not been replaced by another.
That evening I learned enough of the general layout of the
departure wharf to be of good value to me when I came to leave.

Next morning when I tipped the hotel valet, an old man, with
English notes, he fell to his knees and kissed my hand. I said a
final good-bye to Tanya in the Torgsin shop in the hotel, beside
the same little prayer-rug where we had first met.

'You think I am going to cry; that I'm concerned only with a
pattern of silly ideologies. A girl can dream in Russia as well as
anywhere else.' She struck her clenched fist in the palm of her
hand. 'Better, in fact, because here we deal in realities. You think
I have enjoyed your lying silence.' She laughed, it seemed to me,
a little bitterly, then lifted her eyes in that candid gaze which I
had come to like so much and was seeing for the last time. 'You
forgot too often that I was your official guide.'

'You mean I didn't ask sufficient questions.'

'You asked no questions . . . or none that I wanted to answer
. . . and now it is too late.' I was learning fast that in most things

I was to be too early or too late. The next moment she had gone. But it was not easy to dismiss the thought of her from my mind. At each farewell I was still young enough to die a thousand deaths, each tender memory was a little dagger in my side. But now there were other things to be considered.

My plan was to smuggle the fur coat past rather than through the Customs. Paying off the Lincoln, I entered the white and green Torgsin store I had located the previous night.

Every kind of thing was sold there, including rugs from the Caucasus and the southern borders of Russia. In one corner they were piled high and laid out for customers to choose from. While other travellers were busy purchasing goods I casually threw the coat among a pile of rugs and laid one of them over it.

I could see that the door onto the wharf was open and that travellers who had already passed through the Customs could re-enter by it. I found a porter to take my baggage and I passed through Police and Customs after declaring a few purchases and showing my receipts and exchange notes.

Once safely through I sent the porter on to the ship with my baggage and re-entered the Torgsin store by the wharf entrance. My precious coat was still there. I picked it up and went aboard. It had worked; in Russia, I had already learned, behind the outward appearance of efficiency there was the *laissez-faire* casualness of an oriental state.

Though I was on a Russian ship and still in Russia, as we passed the island of Kronstadt my spirits rose at the thought of England and the security of being where I belonged. The voyage home, if not eventful, was delightfully unusual. A nor'wester took charge as soon as the pilot had been dropped. Under a dark, starless sky and a swiftly rising sea the *Smolny* went through every trick she had in her locker. She tossed and rolled and dipped with faithless irregularity. Her deck-chairs left the ship at frequent intervals, her doors and ports joined in the elemental chorus of drum-fire banging. Loosely tied davits swung inwards and broke saloon windows; the ship's crockery was scattered everywhere; her thirty-five passengers were thrown from their bunks, gasping and retching. There seemed to be no sign of stewards, stewardesses or crew. I suppose there must have been a man at the wheel.

Someone asked me anxiously: 'The cargo – will it shift?'

'I can't say for certain; I didn't trim it myself,' I answered unkindly.

Eventually three passengers formed a deputation to see the captain. At the time he was seated at a table in the saloon. Would it not be possible, they suggested, for the ship to alter course? From the far side of the saloon I watched his plate of herrings sliding away from him – there were no fiddles on the table – as he seemed to consider their proposition. Then, to my surprise, he called up the two stewards, the first engineer and one of the stewardesses. After a short consultation it was agreed to alter course slightly. The deputation withdrew and the captain, with a sharp movement, rescued his plate as it was about to tip into his lap. That night, as if by magic, the storm abated.

A few days later, on a bright moonlit night, I watched the two leaves of Tower Bridge rise and open to let us through. There were no Customs working that night, so no one was supposed to leave the ship, but when I explained that I wanted to use the telephone on the wharf I was allowed to go ashore.

From the telephone-box I could see that the dock-gate was ajar so, wasting no time, I walked out with my magnificent Persian coat. I picked up a taxi and drove home. My wife was entertaining. I could see her guests through the glass door of the drawing-room. I don't know if it was because I had been spending so much time recently with serious thinking people or with a people oppressed and searching in vain for the truth, but I was suddenly filled with a feeling of revulsion at the world of pleasure in which my wife and I moved and in which I had been so much at home. I opened the door angrily, flung the coat into the room and left with no further greeting.

The same taxi drove me back to the wharf. I went aboard, lined up a few gifts to declare to the Customs the following morning, climbed into my bunk and slept.

Next day I told my wife that my mind was made up. I was beginning to realise that life is not unlike a sleepless bed;

whichever course you choose you resemble the invalid who turns over, then turns back on finding the second position no better than the first.

I discussed my decision with Father. There were pools of silence in our conversation, as was habitual when he was pursuing a train of thought to its ultimate conclusion. When he concentrated, which he could do at any time and in any company, he would lean back in his chair as motionless as a man sitting for his portrait. Eventually he nodded his head. I knew that he understood me and I knew that he would agree, but he warned me that, in fairness to my brothers and sisters, he could not finance me beyond the more-than-adequate allowance he already paid me.

I intended to go to sea – not to forget by joining a kind of *légion étrangère*, but rather to remember and to experience. I wanted to watch the sun rise and set in a thousand countries; I wanted to be part of wherever my voyages took me.

This parting with my wife was the beginning of a lingering farewell which was to stretch over many months. I felt a pang of sorrow. We had loved each other because we were young, because she was lovely and because we went out with the same friends to the same parties in the same places. I had even fought for her in the first place because there had been a charming naval officer on the scene, Jack Reed, who was already a friend and was to remain so all my life in London, Rio and Cannes.

Anyone who thinks that if he wants to go to sea all he has to do is to find a ship will be disappointed. Even thirty years ago you had to belong to a union, and joining after the age of eighteen is not easy.

I used all the influence I could muster, and of this I was never short; so eventually I became the proud holder of a card in the Sailors' and Firemen's Union and, in due course, I was signed on as an ordinary seaman on the *Highland Pride*, trading between London and Buenos Aires and calling at Rio de Janeiro. She was one of the first refrigerated ships built to carry meat home from the Argentine. The Assistant Marine Superintendent instructed me where and when to join the ship and the best place to buy my

'donkey's breakfast', which, I learned, was the mattress I would
sleep on.

In the motionless frame of memory I see myself standing in the
hall at Ennismore Street, before the glass front door encased in
its lacework of wrought iron, in my hand a cheap canvas hold-all.
As I turn the key it is as if I am holding the very latchkey of the
universe, and then I step out into the street. I must have paused
before I walked from the house because each room and every
corner of it had been part of my life. I must have looked up at the
neat white frontage. It was a place where I had spent long days
and months and years; a place of laughter and tears and careless
loving, yet it had never been a home. The time spent there had
been a chapter of wasted words and the house had been no more
than the location where I had lived too well for too long.

How could I explain just how I felt when I was certain of one
thing only? The time had come for me to be kicked around. Only
that way, I believed, could I marry my imagination to experience
and my reverie to reality. I wanted to see the true colours of life,
the whites, the greys, the blacks and the purples. At last I was to
taste the great tastes and smell the great smells that the world had
to offer.

In my canvas bag I had packed two jerseys, a pair of spare
trousers, socks, etc., which made up my wardrobe, except for the
essential yellow oilskins and a few books.

I was to join the ship the following day, but I went straight
down to the docks in order to cut myself adrift gradually from
the past, and surrender myself to this other world into which I
was deliberately moving.

I first saw Bill leaning against the wall of the Seamen's Mission.
He was watching everything about him with that casual scrutiny
which I was to learn later was characteristic of the seafarer. I
spoke to him and we drifted into the Globe Tavern. It transpired
that he, too, had signed on the *Highland Pride*. This man was to
be a good friend to me in the months ahead, and I can never be
too grateful to him. I wanted a cheap bed for the night, so he
directed me to a house in one of the dim streets that border the
East India Docks.

When the front door was eventually opened I was assailed by a reek of cabbage and greeted by a faded blonde. She told me that I could have the third floor back, to which I climbed, preceded by a little girl, aged about fifteen. In the room the child stood silently watching me as I unpacked my hold-all.

'What's your name,' I asked.

'Mabel Smith,' she replied.

'And do you go to school?'

'Yes, to the one in Standing Street.'

'And what are you going to do when you grow up?'

The child touched her lips with the tips of her fingers, a childish action full of mystery: 'My Mother says when I'm old enough I can be a whore.'

Fortunately, at that moment, from the bowels of the house where the cabbage was announcing its ghastly function, we heard her mother's voice screaming: 'May-bel, May-bel.'

14

Voyage of Discovery

My first voyage in August 1925, was not of the happiest, but it was the most interesting because it enclosed me in an alien world; yet I knew that I was leading a spurious existence. Though I tried to persuade myself that I was part of the life about me, I was really only an observer.

For the first time in my life I was among men whose lives and those of their families depended on their labour. Without help or favour from influential quarters they stood firmly on their own feet. I, on the other hand, knew that money (which can settle so many problems) was always available to me. I had only to send a cable from any part of the world and I knew that help would be forthcoming. It was a way of cheating life, and only the future would reveal the price I had to pay.

Our sleeping quarters on the *Highland Pride* were in the fo'c'sle. This was just what I wanted; now I was truly sailing before the mast, even if it was not in a windjammer. Bill gripped my arm and pushed me for'ard. 'Down there is where we sleep, mate; and eat, mate.' The fo'c'sle was lined with bunks clamped to the ship's sides like double coffins. We threw down our mattresses in two that were unoccupied. Already the old hands were settling themselves in, unpacking and relocking their tin boxes and shifting their gear. The air was already charged with the reek of stale tobacco and the sour smell of sweating feet; I quickly found my way on deck.

Under my feet the ship was already alive. I steadied myself and ran my hand along the smooth teak of the rail and gripped it, seeking to establish that I too was alive and not living a dream.

We had sailed on the evening tide and now we were ploughing through the waters of the estuary with the sun setting behind the low line of the Kentish hills and the gulls circling and sweeping alongside the ship. Twice Bill came for me to go below, but I wanted to experience the moment of departure to the exclusion of all else.

Suddenly, a heavily built man gripped me by the shoulder and twisted me round. In the twilight I was conscious that his eyes were appraising me.

'Turn in,' he ordered abruptly. 'You'll need all the sleep you can get on my ship.' I knew instinctively that this was the bosun, clearly not a man to argue with. Yet in all my sea-going experience I never met a bosun who was the bully so often described in stories of the sea.

I lay awake in my bunk until late in the night. I had heard that musical people are reputed to snore. If this was true my shipmates had the makings of a symphony orchestra, much augmented.

That morning I had been detailed to help bring aboard boxes of butter and sacks of potatoes. I was unused to lifting and carrying, and I burned up energy at twice the rate of my shipmates. There is a knack of co-ordinating the muscles to the exact demands of the job so that none is wasted. Generations of toil behind my shipmates had conditioned them, and they knew instinctively how these heavy weights should be handled. The actual work on board was never to be excessively hard, except when we were put on to the loading and unloading of stores, which was not too often. I soon learned that there was always someone ready to show me how to do a job, and someone who enjoyed doing it for me, as long as I was prepared to stand by watching with an expression of lively admiration. I was already up to my old tricks.

I was issued with a tin plate and mug, a knife, fork and spoon. These had to be handed in at the end of the voyage or the cost was deducted from your pay cheque. Our food was carried over the long stretch of deck between numbers one and two hatch in all weathers by the deck boy always known as

Peggy. He was abused by the galley staff when he went for it and abused in lusty Shakespearean language by the crew when he returned with it – apart from his unwelcome reception at either end he had to negotiate the often slippery decks in all types of weather at seven and eight bells.

Breakfast consisted of porridge, in all climates (guaranteed to give prickly heat in the tropics), on which we sprinkled, very carefully, sugar from our sparse ration. A tin of condensed milk, even when punctured with the smallest holes, was shared with the cockroaches that swarmed in brown-jacketed masses everywhere in the fo'c'sle. The bosun and P.O.s, in addition to the porridge, were each given a bloater. The midday meal was usually salted beef or a sinister stew, which we called by the uninviting name of lobscouse. On Fridays we had fish from Iceland, where it had been kept salted in ice for several seasons. This we knew as bacalão, and it required a resharpening of knives before it could be consumed; to make it more palatable, or to disguise it, the mess was covered with an indescribable sauce known as 'Jessie's dream'. The puddings, liberal in quantity if not quality, were spotted dog and apple waddy. Supper was all the left-overs of the officers' mess, crouching under a thick spread of dough. The Board of Trade ration of lime juice was issued out of large stone jars as soon as we entered the tropics. Truly we ate to keep alive, for there could have been no other reason.

But this was the first night of many in a life that I came to love, a vocation on which my heart was – at least at that time – set. I was to hear the grandest of all voices, the great voices of the sea, and I was to become a wanderer on its surface, visiting strange cities in which to be sad and lonely and wanton and gay.

My shipmates accepted me with easy tolerance. They were by no means the band of brothers that I had expected. Each man seemed to be living independently of the other. There were long discussions which only occasionally developed into a quarrel. Fights rarely took place, and when they did it was invariably the result of a visit ashore. We were bound together only to the same extent as waiters working in a restaurant-car are united on a long-distance train. Many were making their first voyage in this ship and when they signed off would probably join another. Most of the time they behaved towards each other with a quiet tenderness, but in tropical heat the tension grew and a quarrel might start within a second, like the snap of an ivory fan closed in anger; but I was able to read and write without being disturbed, and there was never an occasion when a man wouldn't help me. It was as if I was being mothered until I had learned enough to be on my own.

It was only the atmosphere which at first I found intolerable; the smell of stale, cheap cigarette smoke, the continuous snoring of the night, the mucus-hawking of the morning.

My life became the life of the fo'c'sle, my home was the ship, whether the sun was blistering the decks or great seas hammering against her plates. She was the mother to whom we all returned.

On the *Highland Pride* it was impossible to open the portholes in heavy seas, so that at times the air in the fo'c'sle became un-endurable. One night the first officer found me sleeping on deck. I had been driven there by the stench, of which I was part, and he ordered me back to my bunk. Next day he warned me of the lunatic consequences of sleeping under a tropical moon, especially when it was at the full. In spite of this on several nights I awoke to discover myself on deck. I had climbed the companionway in my sleep.

I told Bill about this and he suggested that I should secure my ankle to the bunkpost, but still I woke up walking on deck as before. So he himself tied me up with better results, though several times I awoke to find myself battling with his Gordian knot. I was warned that I was suffering from a form of calenture, a tropical illness that impels sailors to leap into the sea.

Bill remained with the ship for several voyages, though he preferred the North Atlantic routes. We usually went ashore together. There was a sameness about all the little Caribbean ports. Each had its red-light district with its dust and dirt and, during the rains, its slime and sewage and its perpetual reek of cheap perfume and roasting meats, but worse than this were the malignant and hidden smells, the stench of years of accumulating refuse and excrement, which came alive only at night.

Here we were greeted by women of all breeds, Creole Negresses, Creole whites, Indo-Japanese, pure-blooded Indians and slant-eyed Chinese. They would beckon over the half-doors of their shanties, breasts billowing above and feet showing below. Here we looked into bold black eyes distended with belladonna in sockets white, ebony-black and matt-yellow.

'Come on, Jack. Come on, sailor.' Push our way in and the little silk shawls about their shoulders would fall to the floor. There was a simplicity about it, not without tenderness. They showed what they had to offer and it was just a question of your approval. Sailors were welcome guests in their shanties.

In the large cities and the great ports there were usually Sailors' Missions, where we could read and write letters, but even in the great ports we rarely met female company other than the whores. For us there was only the hospitality of the 'love district'. Here in the sound of automatic music, the night-chatter of the crickets, and the glimmer of fireflies, we were at home. We called for beer, and an almond-eyed girl adorned with little more than a string of amber beads would bring it.

If we had no cigarettes we sent out for more, and another little sister would bring the Luckies or Camels. It was not lust that guided our steps; we were in search of companionship. We looked at hands that were soft and white or yellow or black. To us who had for so long seen only the dirt-ingrained hands of stokers, trimmers and ourselves, they seemed almost transparent in their delicacy. The warm muskiness was luxurious and voluptuous. The tepid beer was nectar and the company gay, but Bill would shake his head whenever one of the girls whispered in his ear, for though he was free with his dollars he was mean with his loving. In this and other ways Bill's life differed from mine. He had learned already; but I was still under tuition, and he was able to pass without hesitation by the doors that for me stood too invitingly open.

How often we must have walked back to our ship in a blue darkness splashed with light that came from under and over the doors, or filtered through the beaded curtains; and reached the quayside only just in time to see the splendour of green moonlight fading before the sun should rise. In the fo'c'sle, as always in port, we were immediately greeted by the all-pervading and unmistakable sour, sharp stench of men who have been drinking and copulating.

On one voyage the ship had tied up in the South Dock, Buenos Aires. This was in the centre of the notorious Boca district, a quarter of the city at that time given over almost enitrely to brothels and sleazy cafés. It was always a dangerous district for the average seaman, the natural prey of every dockside thief, pimp, barman and harlot. With nowhere else to go when we left our ships, we were there for the picking. Stripped of everything, bodies of naked sailors were often fished out of the foetid waters of the South Dock. Walking the streets of the assassins was the sailor's occupational hazard.

On this trip to the Boca I was accosted by a beggar outside a café. I slipped him a few pesos: the Old Man had given me an advance that didn't at all err on the side of extravagance.

In the café I was enjoying a glass of beer when the same man started begging at the different tables. When he came to mine, having already made my contribution, I naturally waved him away, whereupon he drew a knife and struck at me.

Pandemonium broke out. The Latin, who understands reason, responds quite irrationally to violence. A shot was fired and knives were out; suddenly, the lights – already dim – were doused. A second later in the darkness we knew that the *vigilantes* had arrived and were among us like a pack of terriers. I found myself bundled, with a dozen others, into a police-van, and a few minutes later we were emptied not too gently into a prison yard. From here we were driven like cattle into a large cell which I soon realised was the well-known calaboose.

There were at least thirty of us, most having been rounded up in the same café. I sorted out a couple of old hands who explained that we would be kept there until we were brought up for the trial, which might be tomorrow or next month.

The fact that I was entirely innocent, even though the trouble had started with me, impressed none of my fellow-prisoners. If there was trouble in the Boca it was the custom for the *vigilantes* to take everyone in and any sorting out to be done could be effected later in the court before the judge. That night I managed to get a message back to the ship.

Next morning we were arraigned in court. I saw Pepe, a Spanish sailor from the ship, engaged in a violent dispute with the judge. This filled me with surprise, mixed with alarm; I realised that he had been sent to act as interpreter and, unfortunately, though he certainly spoke his own language fluently, his command of English was something of a joke on board. During the hearing of the case he kept turning to me, speaking what he probably believed was English, but the questions he put to me were unintelligible. I became increasingly alarmed when he addressed the judge with a torrent of words, because I knew he hadn't the vaguest idea of what had happened to me.

At one o'clock the judge retired for lunch and we were allowed in the open yard. Our jailers were playing pelota against a lizard-haunted wall. A ball came in my direction and instead of returning it to the players I hit it with a spin against the wall, as Father had taught me to do at fives. The two *vigilantes* were delighted and invited me to play with them. My hands were tough, and I was able to return as hard a ball with my bare hand as they with their gloves.

After a few games, they went over to the man on the gate and I saw them deep in conversation. A minute later they made unmistakable signals to me to vamoose.

Many years later, when I was a King's Messenger, I walked down to the same district and eventually located the prison-yard and the gate through which I had so speedily passed; and I recognised the café where I had afterwards found Pepe on that distant morning, when he had nearly fallen off his chair with surprise to see me making my exit through the calaboose gate.

Our ship, he told me, had sailed for Ensenada where she was loading, so we caught the next train and I reported to the chief officer. Ensenada, on the River Plate, where the great *frigoríficos* were situated, smelt savagely of fresh carcases, which I found very disturbing to my senses. Fortunately the first officer and the bosun took a lenient view of my first voyage adventure, especially when they heard how I had walked out of the calaboose. I did not tell them that in doing so I had lost my money and my few possessions: the jailers had relieved me of them.

Another evening I went ashore on pleasure bent (the ship was about a mile off a small Cuban sugar-port) and I did the usual round of the bars, drinking rum-punches and swizzles fresh with lime; and then, missing the last lighter out to the ship, the rooms at the local brothel being fully occupied, was forced to take one in the leading hotel.

In the great bed, which occupied practically the whole room, I was at once and unmistakably being eaten alive by something. When I turned the light on to investigate I saw that every time I turned over I must have killed whole platoons of bugs, making the sheet look like a red polka-dot counterpane.

After great difficulty I managed to wrench open the rusty bolts of the main door and let myself on to the street. Outside stood a line of open railway-trucks, extending the length of the street. I climbed into one of these and spent an uncomfortable, though cleanly, night, disturbed only by the local *vigilante* who from time to time flashed a light on me. He knew that I had booked a room at the hotel because he had been drinking with me previously, and he seemed astonished that I should prefer the planks of a sugar-truck to the soft comforts of a bed.

Next morning, a great clanking woke me up to the fact that the train was in motion. I climbed out rapidly. The first lighter was leaving for the ship, and boarding it, I lay comfortably on my back on the laden sacks, looking up into the sky, inhaling the quayside smell (a tangy mixture of rope, rum and cigars) and watching the morning light spreading from the east, where its splendour was heralded by hundreds of shooting stars. When we came alongside my body was already hot from the sun's rays, and as I pulled myself up I found that through my thin tropical suit I had melted the sugar in the sacks. Thus syrup-coated, it was as a human *marron glacé* that I appeared before my shipmates, men unaccustomed to such luxuries.

In my travels I often drifted into the shadows of the under-world, the red-light districts, the bordello areas and so-called love-quarters of foreign ports where every woman was for hire to any passer-by who had the money to pay for her loveless embrace. Yet there was always the proud little artist among them, who could dissemble her love-play so that a seaman, against his judgement, because he wanted to, would be half believing in her loving ways, for a man a long time away from home will forget his loneliness and those he loves in the wanton embrace of a European girl or the expert service of an Asiatic doll.

But there were also the semi-professional areas that surrounded the established whore-houses where the rules of the game were adapted to suit the customer. At Recife after dark we drank our rum outside, in the café's garish lights, and girls with flashing smiles would come to the table, naked under their cotton dresses, which they would lift above their breasts, bobbing little convent curtseys, to tempt us to their homes. There was Lily the old Barbadian washerwoman, who came on board with a bevy of coloured girls, ostensibly to carry away the laundry baskets. My captain warned me that as many stayed in your cabin as the shirts you laid out to be washed. It was all very charming and casual and gay. I once saw sisters in Zanzibar being powdered down by their mother, and it was difficult for me and my shipmates not to laugh because they looked as if they had fallen into a flour bin; so that we could occupy the beds, she and her husband had slept on the floor in the hall, and next morning the old grandmother, who had laundered our shirts, brought them into the room ready to wear and crisp and white like the snow on St Wenceslas's day.

How different from the professional hospitality dispensed at the closely shuttered mansion of Madame Safto in Panama or at the mirror-ceilinged establishment in the Rue Caumartin presided over by Madame Floris.

When I suspected my steps would lead me adventuring, I would go with gifts, for a girl never looks more charming than when she holds a present that you have given her; as she examines the fine cambric of the handkerchief or admires the

enamel on the little box, and smooths out the ribbon on the roses
you can watch the expression in her eyes and follow the play of
her hands; money, the necessity, must be relegated to purse or
hidden quickly in stocking-top, but the secret gifts she holds and
caresses in her hands, for they are hers to possess. Already they
are part of her and in some strange way she has become part of
you, because she may remember you, and this can lift the heart
in you, for there's no curse on anything you do as long as
kindness comes first, and you let your heart go free.

A strange episode on one of my voyages persists in my memory. Strange, I suppose, because it was as meaningless as the
shadow of a dream. I had signed on a small ship trading between
the islands. One night I was aroused by quarrelling voices outside
my quarters amidships. We carried deck passengers who slept
wherever they could find space to lie. I went to investigate and,
as I stepped over the bodies, a young girl stood up and pointed
to someone stretched out on the deck.

She said something angrily in a strange lisping French *patois*
which I didn't completely understand. Then, very slowly with
lowered voice, looking me straight in the eyes, she said: 'Zis man
he vife-handle me.'

As she stood there with the moonlight glistening on her young
body, which was ivory-tinted and naked to the waist, there was a
magnificent dignity about her, and a youthful majesty in the
angry gesture that pointed at the man cringing at her feet. 'Vife-
handle me,' she repeated.

Then she continued addressing the man in a bitter flow of
Dominican or Martiniquais French, and the teeth between her
red lips flashed white like those of a young dog. I took her to my
cabin where she curled up in a corner of the deck and slept. The
following morning before we docked she told me where she
lived.

We spent that day discharging cargo in the shimmering heat.
The work was automatic and instinctive, and after a time I
neither glanced down into the opening of the hold nor up into
the sky as the derrick lifted and swung its cargo over onto the

quayside. My eyes were more often on the little white town hanging on the mountainside, and my thoughts were more often on the girl. It was clear that the little ship would not expose her red unladen belly until the end of the week; West Indian stevedores were not men to be hurried.

Throughout the long sweltering day the merciless sun had burned down on the ship's decks and blistered sides. At last it began its decline behind the mountain, trailing a skirt of cool blue shadow across the harbour. The port officials had left, but the agent was still swilling whisky in the Old Man's cabin when the time came for me to knock off. Now I was to see the girl again. There had been something about our first meeting that had delighted my romantic sense, and I wanted her to set the scene and the play to be acted in the manner of her choosing. I didn't want her to think that I had preconceived ideas about her. Whoever she was I wanted to court her.

I must have realised that I was no romantic figure with blue eyes and fair hair; no knight in shining armour. I was just another ordinary brown-eyed sailor from yet another ordinary ship. But I still wanted to approach her as I would a great lady, great in apprehension or beauty; so I meant to behave in the classical and conventional way, even if she chose to laugh at me.

I had put on my whitest suit and a panama hat I had bought in Guayaquil. When I arrived she was seated in a rocking-chair, motionless with her eyes closed, not in sleep, but like someone deep in thought. I gave her a bouquet of flowers I had bought in the town. I could see that she was pleased. She gave me a glass of rum and lime and accepted my present of cigarettes.

I told her that I had looked forward with gay anticipation to meeting her again; how I had viewed the little town from the deck of the ship, the white, pink and lemon-tinted houses, the patchwork of streets linked with steep steps and the red roofs tumbling down the mountainside to the sea; and that I had been thinking about her all the time.

I had, in fact, hurried to her, pushed my way impatiently through the longshoremen, fishermen, the *canotiers* and the idlers on the dockside and threaded my way through the busy main street where people of all shades of colour were buying and selling and chattering, gossiping and strolling between the flaming flower-stalls and the piled-up fruit. It was more by instinct than by her directions that I found my way to her little shack.

On this first visit she was charmingly serious, talking about nothing in her delightful French, which now seemed very sweet from her lips. She became easier to understand, as I came to know her, when her gestures illuminated and at the same time clarified her speech, so that from a distance one might have known what she was saying. The language of the hands and the expression in her eyes, when they were not closed to indicate resignation, were all revealing, because the hands and shoulders moved in conjunction with the faintest flicker of her lashes or the arching of her eyebrows even to the slow raising of her chin when she couldn't answer my question, or wouldn't. In her unhurried, almost timeless manner she made me feel that my visit was one that need never end, for there was a dreamlike quality about her in her home that I had been unaware of on the ship.

I don't know what happened to my honourable resolutions, nor do I remember when I first took her in my arms, for it was as if she had been there since we first met. But I surrendered to the enchantment of the moment, particularly when I first heard her infectious laugh as I twice fell out of the hammock in which we were lying. She didn't ask me to return; probably she knew already that only a ship due to sail and a very deep flower-blue sea would keep me away from her. She must have been accustomed to brief encounters.

In the days that followed, I hurried from the ship as soon as I could, for I was drawn to her by forces I could not and would not resist. We had no common bond of race or culture; but I would have scaled a precipice to reach her.

Sometimes when I arrived she was bent over the washtub, and the white suds shone like bubbled cream against the honey of her skin. I would stand holding the bead-curtain aside, watching her; and she would turn towards me, her blue-black hair hung back from her little face, and try to remove a soap-sud from her forehead with the back of her hand, and succeed only in leaving another one on her nose. But her dark eyes would gleam and her smile would be rich and mocking.

For the first few days she called me 'sailor'; then one day she asked me, surprisingly, whether I was a Christian. She said that she had never heard of a saint of my name so she called me Juan.

I spent many hours in her shanty, seated in an old rocking-chair under a coloured picture of Our Lady and Child. Sympathy grew between us without any apparent effort, for in some strange way she gave me a feeling of a home and tranquillity.

At that time I was as dark as Othello, and it never ceased to amuse her when she compared her golden skin with mine. In my bunk at night, when I thought of the secrecy and strangeness of her life, I was confronted with an insoluble mystery. It was as if life had made her accept a stranger's love-embrace as having no more significance than changing a record on her poor little gramophone. She probably looked on the money I gave her as a welcome addition to what she earned, but it must never have occurred to her that I was keeping her and that, at least during my short stay, she owed me a gesture of faithfulness.

Yet during the time I was visiting her I never saw another man enter or leave; though sometimes my eyes would be drawn reluctantly to a smoked-out cigarette, and sometimes I would catch the faint but unmistakable smell of ship's tobacco. Though no one ever came to the door, I was conscious that someone had been there and left just before my arrival. She spoke always as if today was yesterday and tomorrow would never arrive.

Twice I had a half-day off, and to anticipate the pleasure of visiting her, I sat by a dilapidated fountain, drowsy and mesmerised by the quivering heat, the silence of the siesta-hour broken only by the occasional notes of a guitar that drifted lazily across the dusty little plaza. I would wait patiently until the narrow street that led to her home was dusky with house-shadows. After the great heat of the afternoon her little room was as cool as green twilight, sweetened with the faint odour of faded rose-water.

Along one wall there were at least twenty pairs of shoes and sandals. Her wardrobe seemed to consist entirely of a large assortment of lengths of cotton in vivid colours. These she wore in turn, in the Taipei fashion, knotted at the side of her waist, leaving a slit from hip to ankle. Above the waist she was bare, and her breasts accentuated the natural grace of all her movements.

Sometimes she behaved as if I were not there. As I watched her lost in her own secret thoughts, there was about her a delicacy and reserve that was in strange contrast to her occasional mood of gay lasciviousness. She could be completely childlike in her unconsciousness of my presence, and at times like these she made no effort to free herself of her thoughts, nor did I wish her to.

There were two sides to her affection. One side was childishly loving, accompanied by natural and caressing gestures; and the other, the uncontrolled sexual hunger of the primitive woman. But at most times there was a dignity and a gentleness about her that was enchantingly sophisticated. Hers was a charm that defied definition.

She never once asked me a question that could have been regarded as personal, nor did she ask me when I would be leaving; and when I did leave she never asked when I would be returning. Early in our friendship I began slipping peso notes in a cedar box resting on the rickety table. I noticed that none of the money seemed to have been spent, for gradually the box was becoming full. When I called her attention to this she immediately took out a note, and grasping my hand, literally dragged me down the dusty street to the stifling square. Here we spent an hour while she tried on one pair of shoes after another. Eventually, she bought a pair with heels so high that she had to take my arm for support on our walk home.

Arrived there, she stepped hurriedly out of them. I too always went barefoot in her place; the floor was shiningly clean and the uncovered tiles were cool under my feet. There was a small patio in the back where she kept bottled beer in a canvas water-bucket, tied by a rope to a blue jacaranda. Every time she passed the tree she touched the bucket to keep it swinging so that I could always have a cold drink.

I never met her in the town nor did I see her standing in her doorway. Who were her clientele? Who paid for her loveless service? I had bought her a kimono in the town which she wore to sleep in, so that I knew when she had been entertaining someone other than myself from the imprint of the string hammock on her young body. Why did they never come when I was there? They must be men of the sea, for had she not called me 'sailor' and talked about pesos as dollars?

The day came when the ship was loaded and ready to sail. I said nothing of this to her, and yet throughout the last afternoon I was conscious of an expression in her searching eyes that I had never seen before. And that evening she walked down to the town with me, something she had never done before. When we reached the quayside she suddenly took off her high-heeled shoes; then, flinging her arms around me, hugged me like a child. It was the last time I was to smell the rose-water in her hair and feel her sad mouth on mine; the next moment she was running out of my life through the violet twilight, leaving a line of little footprints in the dust. Just as the little phrase in Vinteuil's sonata and the taste of the little *madeleines* evoked particular people in Proust's memory, so the distant notes of a guitar and the smell of rose-water always kindle the glowing memory of this little Caribbean girl whose name I have long forgotten.

My ship was bound for Jamaica. The stars grew dim and there was only the ghost of the moon in the sky. The gathering storm broke and the lightning flashed menacingly through the vast curtain of tropical rain that hammered on the decks and flooded the scuppers. A hundred lands lay beyond a limitless horizon and a thousand ports, with the blindfold years stretching ahead and the sailor's farewell whispering in my ears:

> Le temps est beau,
> La mer est belle.
> Doucement je vais
> Au bord d'elle.

I was never to return to that little port, but I can never forget her and the air of mystery that enveloped her and masked her thoughts; nor can I forget the chill of loneliness that ran down my spine as I had pulled myself up the gang-plank. She had taught me that in all human beings the secret places of the heart and the dark places of the mind are rarely revealed, and I felt a strange sense of gratitude towards her because she had taught me unconsciously a little more about myself. Already I was learning that there are as many shades between right and wrong as there are between black and white, and that no man can exist outside his dreams and his imagination.

15

Voyage not Completed

IN every ship I have sailed in I would hear the story, ever-
green, like that of the Spanish Prisoner, of the lonesome
sailor who is walking the waterfront of a foreign port when
an enormous car pulls alongside him. He is invited to enter and
then, with blinds drawn, he is driven to a splendid mansion in
Marseilles, a vast palace on the Bosporus or a discreet harem in
Alexandria. Here a butler, a major-domo or a eunuch escorts
him to a fabulous bedroom, where, on a glistening satin bed,
there lies the most beautiful woman he has ever set eyes on.
Delicious food and sparkling decanters of wine are on a side-
table, and there in dalliance, feasting and loving, he spends the
most glorious twenty-four hours of his life. Then the car with
the drawn curtains drives him back to the waterfront.

Every sailor knows the story; indeed, most sailors tell it about
themselves at some time. Yet each listens enraptured as it is
repeated, just as children never tire of the story of Cinderella. If
explanations are requested, which is rare, it is invariably main-
tained that the beautiful lady's husband – sultan or sheik – was
impotent, and that a son and heir was in urgent demand.

My homecoming from my first voyage was as pleasant as any
sailor could dream. On my arrival home my wife was standing
in the drawing-room in front of the window. The chiffon curtains
hung in cascading pleats, reflecting the winter sunlight in
festooning folds of amber and white with an occasional gleam
of silver lacing the texture. There was a log fire burning, and
the room was full of flowers and Guerlain's *l'heure bleue*.

However much she liked to see me leave, I was persuaded that she was always pleased to see me return. Parties and dinners followed at Ciro's or the Berkeley, with visits to the night-clubs – the Quadrant, the Florida, the Embassy, the Four Hundred – ending up with a breakfast of hot strong sweet tea and fragrant kippers at the cab-shelter at Hyde Park Corner, known to initiates as the Junior Turf Club. Just as some people are creatures of the day, my wife, like the flower that gives off its perfume at night, seemed to wake up only when darkness fell.

That first evening at home I would have preferred to have spent alone with her, but when I returned later and stepped into the drawing-room I was greeted by the lively music of popping corks and an atmosphere laden with cigarette-smoke and *l'heure bleue*. I knew then that I was ferociously back home.

Someone hailed me with a glass of champagne in one hand and a brandy in the other, a cigar was thrust between my teeth. A girl grabbed my carnation for her boy-friend's buttonhole, and someone shouted: 'Where's your parrot, sailor?' A gramophone was singing:

> Money buys anything but love:
> I've been poor and I know which is which,
> And I'd sooner be rich.

My return had been made the reason for the party, but I felt I belonged nowhere in it. I knew none of the current jokes. I was no longer interested in social gossip, and I was sufficiently sensitive to realise that I was not even good company. Bronzed and slightly barbaric, I was an eccentric and a freak. I remembered a song sung in the New York Bar:

> He was the life and soul of the party
> But he's a dumbell when he's at home.

That was me.

I realised that our marriage was over and only the sad farewell remained to be said. We had married just after the war, before young people had become adjusted to the hazards of peace. We had all escaped from a world of vast and violent uncertainty into one of pleasure and security, yet it became a prison, out of which I was now breaking. And now I wondered whether we had ever said anything to each other that even mattered. In the final farewell we were, perhaps, closer spiritually than we had been over the years of marriage. I was learning that new sorrows bring new depths of experience.

There were the sad little questions, the do-you-remembers. Did she remember the time in Monte Carlo when I went ahead with one of our guests and 'bancoed' a player who was usually unlucky, and I lost, and play at the table was held up because she had all the money in her bag? She strolled into the room, and when I asked her for a hundred francs she said: 'No, you'll only lose it', and everyone at the table laughed, and even the croupier smiled as she slowly understood and reluctantly produced the money. And the night on our honeymoon when the drunk man came into our room, and our irrepressible laughter when he got onto the second and unoccupied bed and snored the whole night through and was still asleep when we left the room next morning?

Did she remember when we were walking in the gardens of the Alhambra? So easy for me to recall because of the perfume of the jasmine petals she was carrying in her little hand, and because of the exquisite moment when suddenly we heard the subtle, almost subterranean music of Falla's *Nights in the Gardens of Spain*, floating into the moonlight.

Now there was nothing I wanted. I wanted no possessions; the house was to me no more than a place I had loved and dreamed in. I was never to return there, nor was I ever to see her again with the sunset in her eyes and the haunting breath of *l'heure bleue* in the air.

This I did know: I was in danger of drifting back to a life of soft living. I must keep moving, and I knew that the time had come for me to sign on another ship. The night before I sailed, we ran into Bertie Hollender, an old friend and a well-known character in the bohemian and racing world of London. He persuaded us to visit a night club, which was already closed.

After a little persuasion the waiter was induced to bring us three large whiskies. The bill when I received it was over four pounds, which I considered excessive; and, conscious that my days of extravagance were over, I gave the waiter two pounds, which I considered adequate, whereupon he complained, pointing to the bill. 'What about the balance?' So I signed the bill with the signature Davy Jones and instructed him to take it away and put it in his locker.

The next day I signed on the *London Exchange* sailing out of the London docks for the U.S.A. with Philadelphia as the first port of call, then New York, Boston and home. Although I did not know it, it was to be my last voyage. The weather in the Atlantic was one long westerly gale, through which we fought our way with life-lines along the deck and hatches battened down. A man could have leaned against that wind without falling; it was like an invisible wall.

At one time we were hove-to in mid-Atlantic; it was the first time I was genuinely frightened at the immensity of the seas, which seemed at every moment about to engulf us. They towered above and surrounded us; but each time, just before they broke, the bows rose and the ship righted herself. For one moment she hung above the limitless vision of mountainous seas, only to be swept and sucked the next second into an eighty-foot cauldron. It was awe-inspiring, unforgettable.

In the fo'c'sle we were strangely silent, each occupied with his own thoughts. We lay hove-to for three days; then the seas abated and we continued the voyage, sighting the Ambrose Light seventeen days outward-bound from London. It was the ship's first voyage under the command of a new and young master. He was not more than thirty-four, and in the fo'c'sle the men were whispering that the voyage boded ill for either ship or master. Which would it be? This was the unspoken question all were asking. The night we berthed, I went ashore in Philadelphia, having arranged to meet Mac (the third engineer) at a near-by saloon. At 11 o'clock he had still not appeared. It was an understood thing among sailors that no man should return to the ship alone, for this meant crossing a vast and ill-lit goods yard. It was not unusual for homing sailors to be held up by one of the Delaware gangs; gunmen who appeared suddenly from behind the stationary trucks, coshed or shot their victim and stripped him of everything, then dumped the body in the river. In the dimness a man needed to give his full attention to crossing the rails, to say nothing of being on the look-out for these gangs, expert as they were in all the tricks of midnight ambush.

I drank in the saloon until midnight, with no sign of Mac. So, weary of waiting, I started back to the ship without him. Very cautiously I negotiated my way between the trucks. I had drunk with caution and I was alone, which gave me two advantages – I could take my own time, and one man makes less noise than two. There were shadows all about me, some wavering, some still, but I felt instinctively that I was being stalked. Gradually I made my way through the trucks until there was only one line of them left between me and the ship. Everything seemed quiet enough except for the night sounds of a great river and a sort of breathing movement among the trucks. They were motionless, but it was only as though in sleep and not in death. There were small sounds, difficult to distinguish; the muffled tap-tap of a hanging chain or an uneasy connecting-rod, or was it footsteps? Someone, I felt, was creeping up on me.

At the exact moment that I realised that there was a man beside me a shot rang out. Instinctively I rushed for the trucks. The next moment I was on the ship's gang-plank and safe. It was then, and only then that I realised that the shot must have come from on board.

I raced for the saloon; lights were blazing. The body of the captain lay on the deck between the tables with the top of his head blown off. Then suddenly the first officer appeared and a second later the whole ship came to life. Already the saloon was impregnated with the rancid smell of blood.

The two hours that followed were among the most disagreeable in my life. Sirens wailed and the police came swarming in. I was immediately hustled to a cabin and put under third degree. I had to explain all my movements from the time I had gone ashore. Grimly they suggested that it wasn't usual for a sailor to go back to his ship without a shipmate. I explained the reason, but couldn't confirm it until Mac returned.

I had already realised that the mate could give no other evidence than that he had heard a shot fired and rushed to the saloon, where he found me even before he saw the body. It was possible, he had to agree, that I might have been present when the captain died. My position was a tricky one; yet how could they tie a motiveless murder on me?

Later, Mac came aboard, and, unaware of the tragedy, found himself under immediate interrogation. His reply to their first question was 'Well, I've not been with a whore, if that's what you are thinking.'

The ship was due to sail that night, and all preparations were under way. At last the police made ready to leave and the body was carried ashore. I was released, but with the warning, 'When we want you we'll know where to find you.' The mate handed them a letter which the captain before his death had placed among those to be taken ashore by the pilot.

There was an uneasy silence throughout the ship as we headed through the night for New York. The crew's unspoken questions had been answered and their premonitions fulfilled. Although none suspected me of the murder, if murder it was, I had nevertheless the feeling that all looked on me as the harbinger of death, a Jonah about whom there hung an indefinable aura of misfortune.

Standing my watch at the fo'c'sle head, with the passing of each half-hour I would hail the bridge: 'Your lights are burning bright, sir!' And back would come the faint wind-tossed reply, as though it were the ghost-voice of the dead man himself: 'Ri–ight! Ri–ight!'

I felt seized by profound melancholy. The uneasy silence in the fo'c'sle that had met me as I came down the companion-way when the police had let me go, and my shipmates' uneasy glances now, seemed suddenly more than I could bear. Staring into the darkness of the long Atlantic swell I resolved irrationally that I would have no more of it. I would jump ship as soon

as we touched land again. Next morning, the eve of Christmas,
we steered into New York harbour. As we entered we passed a
Norwegian and a Danish training ship, both schooners. They
were under power, having a contrary wind, and their masts
and rigging were frozen over, reminding me of two of Father's
ship models that were each carved out of purest crystal.

The sun shone from the bluest of skies, and the tall buildings
of downtown Manhattan were glowing and flashing reflections
from their thousand windows. In those days the highest sky-
scrapers were downtown, dominated by the Woolworth Building, and because of this the first impression of a high cliff of
masonry reaching up to the clouds was even more impressive
than it is now, when the buildings seem to recede in perspective
towards the heights. The sheer steepness has gone out of it;
it no longer gives the shock-impression, the vision of glass and
steel and concrete, of a perpendicular precipice.

As we came up to our wharf I could see that all the ships'
masts, funnels, stanchions, rails and warps were encrusted in
ice from stem to stern. A dazzling and splendid sight; hundreds
of ships – liners, freighters, tankers, tugs and ferry-boats –
anchored, tied up or under way, all captured in the ice and
glittering in the sun's rays. It was a work of nature that was
different from the trees and meadows and green fields of heavy
winter because it was welded to man's own work and invention.
I had never before thought of nature as brittle, metallic and
scintillating.

We had arranged that Mac would meet me with my suitcase
at the Seamen's Mission on the Battery, as I did not wish to be
seen leaving the ship with a bag. As I stepped ashore, with utter
despair in my heart, I knew that I had come to the end of
another chapter in my life. I had jumped my ship; something I
shall regret to the end of my days.

I had ten pounds in my pocket, and I meant to have a good
Christmas evening downtown or uptown, for in those days the
pound was worth nearly five dollars and prices had not risen
with the buildings. In England five shillings was still referred
to as a dollar.

I wasn't surprised when Mac, who met me as arranged, refused to spend the evening with me. I have never met a mean Scotsman. I have met careful ones, but never one who did not pay his corner if he was in it. Mac was saving up to get married; he was not going to spend money he could save, and he was not going to let me pay as long as he had the money. So that was that.

'This is where we came in, Mac.'

'Aye, that's the way it goes. And take my advice and keep awa' from here till the heat's off, for it's here they'll be looking for ye.'

He promised he would call for any letters I might want him to post in England. After he was gone it was a long time before I ceased to feel the grip of his hand in mine. Normally, I am inclined to distrust a man who gives you a killer hand-grip, but I have discovered that there are too many exceptions to everything for a sensible man to be bound too closely to the accepted canons of behaviour. I have met the most honest men with close-set eyes, the most brilliant and determined with runaway chins, and the most generous with small tight-lipped mouths. The most reliable man I ever knew and loved had a flabby handgrip. I asked him about this once and he said: 'The truth is I have hands that perspire, and I don't think it's pleasant for other people.'

As I changed into my evening clothes that night at the Seamen's Mission, I realised that I was not disappointed at being alone. My depression lifted.

I could now play drifter. In an unknown foreign city drifting is one of the greatest games to be played, because things happen to drifters and they are not always unpleasant things. It was not a game that Mac would enjoy, but it was just the game for a lonely man on Christmas Eve, so long as he was dressed for any part.

Feeling in my pocket, as one does when one changes into another suit, to my delight and amazement, in the trouser hip I discovered a beautiful twenty-five-pound note. When, later, I wrote and told my wife about this delightful surprise, she replied illogically: 'That's why you never had any money.'

The important thing was that I now had money, not only for my evening, but also at least five pounds towards Mac's dream house. Having therefore left an envelope for him, I took a taxi to the Brevort, an hotel in Greenwich Village, where I could stay or leave my bag and be not too far from the Battery. I liked the Brevort. It was the sort of hotel I've been fond of all my life. It is not that I dislike the atmosphere of good-living and carnations and cyclamen mixed with the faint suggestion of fine cooking, such as you may notice in hotels like Claridge's or the Hôtel de Paris, or that I prefer the musty hotels of forlorn palms and crummy antimacassars; I like each in turn, one for enjoyment and the other for comfort, like sunshine and rain. You sit in one and you stand in the other.

The Brevort in those days was a good old-fashioned New York hotel, run more on English lines than on American or Swiss. I felt safe here. No one would search the Brevort for a sailor who had deserted his ship, a police-suspect, without papers of any sort, a stranger in a foreign land. It was at that time a refuge for successful artists and the poor aristocracy of America.

I gave the hall-porter my canvas bag (at which he looked askance), informing him that I might possibly be staying with friends so I would not check in. If I was to stay I preferred to have any official discussions over necessary papers, passport, etc., with the late-duty porter, because I have always found that it is easier to come to terms with creatures of the night than those of the day.

After a large scotch I lit a cigar and wandered from one place to another, in Greenwich Village then took a taxi uptown to 42nd Street and Times Square. Already in the few hours I had been in New York I was in thrall to its breathless vitality. Even the buildings seemed to be alive. One sensed that it was survival of the fittest only, in the world's greatest jungle. I met a friend who had been working only three months in New York.

'How are you doing, Sandy Harvie?' I asked.

'Not so well,' he replied, 'but it's just round the corner, boy, just round the corner.'

Everywhere one feels this wonderful sense of expectation; and besides this, I have always enjoyed the American sense of humour, when it is of the dry variety, which can be found in every state of the Union.

Then I took a taxi to the Plaza. It was a sort of American Claridge's. Here I might feel more at home; and on Christmas Eve a man likes to feel at home every now and then. The hotel was a fine building, built before the height-competition started. It stands at the corner of Fifth Avenue and 59th Street, and one side faces Central Park with the entrance in Fifth Avenue. Here there is a small drive-in with a patch of grass known as Plaza Park. On the Park side I was delighted to see a line of hansom-cabs. I drifted towards it, for a hansom-cab was something I could never resist.

'Take me for a drive,' I said.

'In the Park, sor?' he asked.

'Why would I wish to be driving through a park without a girl beside me, Paddy? Drive me through the streets, my darling man.'

I saw that we had turned down what I thought was Madison Avenue, so I shouted to him: 'Do you pass the Ritz-Carlton?' The reply swift and sure: 'Not if you wish to alight, sor.'

I decided not to pay him off, but gave him enough to quench his Gaelic thirst, and he promised to return for me.

In the hotel, among a throng of people, I sat down to consider my problem. This was as good a place to do it as any, for this was the Ritz with the unmistakable imprint of the great César – the familiar pink-blue-and-yellow pattern on the rugs and carpets, the familiar chandeliers and frozen statuary, the familiar atmosphere. But it was not the Ritz in London or Paris or Madrid or Barcelona; and suddenly I knew for the first time that, however much I might learn to love America, I would always be a European at heart. But now the problem was how to get back to Europe.

I had no passport. I could hardly go to our Consul-General without confessing I had deserted my ship. I could not leave the U.S.A. without a passport. More serious still, I was without any document showing how I had entered the country.

After my second scotch I realised that I was not likely to find the solution to my problems at the Ritz-Carlton. To do that I must seek out a very different world, where things were done outside the law; tomorrow the law might be looking for me. In the meantime it was Christmas Eve and I was alone.

As if my thoughts had been spoken aloud, a young American from a near-by party invited me to join them. 'We've decided you look like a lonely Englishman, if it won't bore you, old boy, and all that,' he said in comic stage English. This was an invitation not to be resisted; the importance of accepting any such offer was high up in the rules of drifter. 'If you can put up with a slow-thinking man, I guess I'd like to,' I replied.

The men were friendly, the girls beautiful, and the old-fashioneds cold and dry and frequent. I suspect they laughed at me, not in an unkindly way, but at that time an Englishman was still a curiosity and a bit of a joke. Why was I wearing a dinner jacket? Was that an amber cigarette-holder? And why did I smoke Turkish tobacco? Was I alone? All dressed up and no place to go?

I explained that I was all dressed up and with lots of places to go, but I could not decide which. This they did not believe; one of them had already telephoned a girl, and a little later we were a party of even numbers (with only one of us wanted by the police). It all happened many years ago, but I would be very surprised if the girl wasn't beautiful; because American women make a habit of being so. Even if she had not been, I would have told her she was, for already I had learned that a woman will accept any deception that comes in the form of flattery. I remember how, in the generous American manner, they refused to let me pay for anything. I could only contribute my share to the party by buying branches of little mauve and white orchids for the girls. While doing this I organised another surprise for them. I sent Paddy to round up three more hansom-cabs. Half an hour later, when we emerged, they were surprised and delighted to find a magnificent cavalcade lined up in the avenue, headed by my jarvey.

We piled in and drove from one bright spot to another, ending in the early hours with a hansom-race round Central Park. It had been a strange evening, a genuine drifter, with a great deal spent, nothing accomplished, and a wonderful time had by all; and this must have included eight hangovers next morning.

I have written that nothing was accomplished during that evening, but apart from the strange and lovely interlude when we attended midnight Mass at St Patrick's Cathedral I had made a useful friend in Paddy.

My tongue being loosened by much wine I told him my predicament. He volunteered to help. Will any Irishman take it amiss if I say that there is not one of them who does not, from time to time, enjoy something slightly nefarious ? It was arranged that we should meet next day. In the meantime he would drive me to the Brevort. Paddy put a bottle of Guinness onto the desk. 'You're a grand man,' he said to the porter; then, noticing me, he added courteously: 'You're both grand men.' And as I stepped into the lift I heard his old voice saying: 'Sure, we're all grand men.'

Next morning I paid my bill and left the hotel. Indeed, my seafaring clothes were quite unsuitable for the Brevort. Paddy was faithful to his appointment, and we drove straight to West Street. Here he parked the cab and directed me to a saloon where I was to wait for him. I was feeling none too well after the party, so he could not have chosen a more suitable place in that grimy district, but after three hours I became seriously alarmed at his protracted absence. The only thing that kept me to the spot and my instructions was the comforting fact that the old horse-and-cab were still there.

When he eventually arrived I could have embraced him. He explained that his contact had not been immediately available, but he had eventually found him and all was well. In short, for eight pounds the man would get me aboard a ship with no questions asked. 'I beat him down,' said Paddy. 'It took an hour, but you can trust him.' I guessed that he had knocked him down by two pounds.

'You've to sleep at Moore's Hotel tonight; he'll call for you at six o'clock tomorrow night; you'll pay him the money and he'll see you aboard.'

After a few drinks to crown the deal Paddy left me with his blessing, but not before he had popped his head round the door and remarked, in the practical manner the Irish can always summon at will: 'You'll fix your passage-money with the captain.'

I found my own way to Moore's Hotel without having to enquire from a passer-by. I never like doing this in New York because everyone seems to be in a hurry, nor have they been told by their parents, as I had by Father: 'Never become abusive when someone asks for a street direction.'

I spent the next day waiting, not without anxiety, for I was afraid to leave the crummy hotel in case the plans were changed. But Paddy's man was on time. He saw me onto the ship and I paid him eight pounds plus the two pounds I guessed that Patrick had knocked him down. I did this because before I had met Paddy I would willingly have paid any man ten pounds to do for me what he had done. Not to do so now I would have regarded as a betrayal of my first intention and, foolishly or superstitiously, I had no wish to be in debt to my fate.

I arranged to pay the master of the ship fifteen pounds on my arrival in London. Nothing more remains to be told of this: my last voyage as a seaman was over. No further charge hung over me. Through a former shipmate I learned that the letter left by the captain of the *London Exchange* proved clearly that he had died by his own hand. My discharge book still lies unclaimed in the Custom House, bearing the words no seaman ever likes to read: 'Voyage not completed'. I was not yet thirty. It was all long ago.

As the train races forward on the hard unyielding track, the drumbeat of the grinding bogies gives place to the hollow echoes of a tunnel as we burrow into the darkness. In the dim green light I gaze up at the ceiling of my compartment, it is rounded like one of Mother's and Father's old leather trunks. My compartment is locked, my 'crossed' bags and my secret dispatches are secure. I am a middle-aged if not staid King's Messenger, off on a routine journey. Like most dogs I have had my day.

It is hard for me, across the still eventful years, to recognise, as the scroll of memory unfolds, the child-boy-man I had been, or believe the kind of world I was born and reared in could ever have existed. Once more I hear beloved voices. I taste the salt on my lips and I smell the familiar tang of the sea.